AMERICA'S FAVORITE WILD GAME RECIPES

CY DECOSSE INCORPORATED

A COWLES MAGAZINES COMPANY

Chairman/CEO: Bruce Barnet
Chairman Emeritus: Cy DeCosse
President: James B. Maus
Chief Operating Officer: Nino Tarantino
Executive V. P. Creative: William B. Jones
AMERICA'S FAVORITE WILD GAME RECIPES
Group Executive Editor: Zoe Graul
Hunting & Fishing Library Director: Dick Sternberg
Book Development Leaders: Ellen Boeke, Peggy Ramette
Contributing Writer: Teresa Marrone
Editors: Janice Cauley, Dick Sternberg
Senior Project Manager: Joseph Cella
Senior Art Director: Delores Swanson
Art Director: Linda Schloegel
Home Economists: Terry McDougall, Peggy Ramette, Mary Kaye Sahli,
  Elizabeth Shedd
Dietitian: Hill Nutrition Associates, Inc.
Vice President of Development Planning & Production: Jim Bindas
Director of Photography: Mike Parker
Lead Photographer: Mike Parker
Creative Photo Coordinator: Cathleen Shannon
Studio Manager: Marcia Chambers
Photographers: Stuart Block, Rebecca Hawthorne, Rex Irmen,
  Bill Lindner, Paul Najlis, Charles Nields, Robert Powers
Contributing Photographers: Mette Nielsen, Brad Parker
Hand Models: Michelle Peterson, Kay Wethern
Styling Director: Bobbette Destiche
Food Stylists: Susan Brue, Bobbette Destiche, Elizabeth Emmons,
  Melinda Hutchison, Nancy J. Johnson, Abigail Wyckoff
Stylist Assistants: Karen Linden, Catherine Schack
Production Manager: Laurie Gilbert
Senior Desktop Publishing Specialist: Joe Fahey
Production Staff: Deb Eagle, Kevin Hedden, Mike Hehner,
  Robert Powers, Mike Schauer, Greg Wallace, Kay Wethern, Nik Wogstad
Consultants: Annette and Louis Bignami; Joan Cone; Gerald Cooper/
  Morton Salt; William Gregoire; Rytek and Tom Kutas/The Sausage
  Maker; Teresa Marrone; John and Denise Phillips; Keith Spencer/
  Hi Mountain Jerky

Library of Congress
Cataloging-in-Publication Data

America's favorite wild game recipes.
p. cm. — (The Hunting & fishing library)
Includes index.
ISBN 0-86573-044-X (hardcover)
1. Cookery (Game) 2. Cookery, American. I. Cy DeCosse
Incorporated. II. Series.
TX751.A45 1994
641.6'91--dc20   94-32784

Contents

2 Tbs.

2 Tbs. Paprika

2 Lbs. Venison Stew Meat 1

3 Tbs. Olive Oil

1 c. chopped onion

clove garlic

Introduction

In 1987, The Hunting & Fishing Library® published *Dressing & Cooking Wild Game.* It offered something unique to the sportsman/cook: a wide variety of exciting, tested recipes, combined with stunning photography and step-by-step sequences for preparing and cooking wild game. The clear photos and written descriptions provided detailed instructions on everything from field-dressing game to home butchering to kitchen procedures. *Dressing & Cooking Wild Game* quickly became one of our most popular titles. And our readers wanted more.

So we're proud to bring you *America's Favorite Game Recipes,* a collection of nearly 150 exceptional recipes for all types of game. To ensure a wide variety of recipes, we tapped a number of different sources: chefs at restaurants known for innovative wild game cookery; veteran outdoor writers; hunting lodges from across the country; and professional food writers. We invited Hunting & Fishing Library subscribers to submit their personal favorites. We even persuaded a few hunting buddies to reveal some camp specialties.

The recipes were then put to the test. Every recipe in this book has been thoroughly tested by home economists to ensure success. Hunting & Fishing Library staffers and friends tasted each dish, too, to help us select only the best recipes.

We've divided this book into sections based on a menu approach. There are sections for appetizers; main dishes; soups, stews and chilies; and a detailed section on sausages and smokehouse specialties. Helpful photo sequences throughout the book show you how to prepare complex recipes, stuff natural and synthetic sausage casings and make jerky. We've also compiled comprehensive substitution charts for each type of game (pages 8 to 13), including helpful general advice on substitutions and information on using domestic meat in place of wild game in recipes.

No matter whether you're a first-time deer stalker, a dedicated waterfowler, or a cook who buys game from a grocery store or game farm, there's sure to be a recipe in this book that will help you savor the incomparable flavors of the wild harvest.

Nutritional Information

Each recipe includes nutrition information and exchanges for weight management. If a recipe has a range of servings, the data applies to the greater number of servings. If alternate ingredients are listed, the analysis applies to the first ingredient listed; optional ingredients are not included in the analysis.

All recipes were tested with the game animal specified, but since nutritional data on some species is not available, appropriate substitutions were made. Analyses of recipes that specify partridge were done with pheasant. Analyses for whole ducks were done with domestic duck data, but recipes that call for duck breast were analyzed with wild duck data. Goose analyses were done with data for domestic geese, which are not as lean as wild geese. The analyses for ground big game are for meat that has been adjusted to have a 20% fat content. Beefalo data was used for buffalo. Other species information is based on USDA figures. Cholesterol figures are not available for a number of game species; this is indicated by the symbol N/A.

Tips for Handling & Cooking Wild Game

After the hunt, it's important to handle game properly to ensure maximum quality. Whether you're cleaning pheasants for the freezer, preparing a special venison dinner, or wrapping up leftovers, the following tips will help you get the most out of your wild harvest.

ORGANIZE your upright or chest freezer so you always know what type of game you have on hand. Buy plastic baskets in various colors, and place a particular type or cut of game in its own color basket. When you need meal ideas, it's easy to see what type of game is plentiful. Always label and date newly frozen meat and place it at the bottom of the basket so that you will use older packages first.

LARD venison roasts before oven roasting to keep them moist. Line the channel of a larding needle with a ¼" strip of pork fat, available from your butcher. Pierce the roast completely with the needle, then pull the needle out while holding the fat in. Repeat as many times as desired, spacing fat strips evenly. For additional flavor, the fat can be seasoned or marinated prior to larding.

EXAMINE the spurs on a rooster pheasant to help determine its age. Long, pointed spurs (top) indicate a mature bird, which should be braised (cooked with liquid at a low temperature). Short, rounded spurs (bottom) indicate a young bird, which can be cooked using any method.

TENDERIZE a mature wild goose by parboiling it prior to roasting. Place the bird in a kettle of cold, salted water. Bring to a boil over medium heat; reduce heat and simmer for about an hour. Remove from water. Pat dry. Roast as usual. The salted water also helps remove blood from shot holes.

WEAR rubber gloves when handling wild rabbits as protection against *tularemia*, or "rabbit fever." Although the possibility of contamination is slim, the rabbit carcass can carry bacteria even after dressing and skinning. Thorough cooking destroys bacteria.

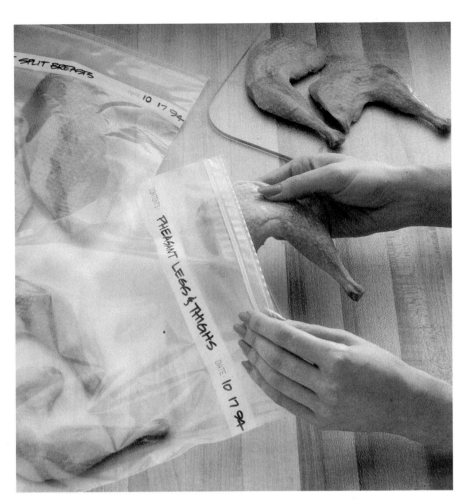

SEPARATE breasts from thighs and legs when freezing cut-up pheasants, ducks or other birds. Then, if your recipe calls for breast meat only, you won't have to thaw the other parts.

USE the leftover carcass of a roasted bird to make stock. Freeze carcass pieces in a heavyweight plastic bag; add additional carcasses until you have enough accumulated to make stock. When boning fresh birds, add the uncooked backbones, thigh bones and leg bones to the bag. They will add additional flavor and richness to the stock.

The above recipe, Johnny Appleseed Pheasant (page 72), works equally well with cut-up pheasant (left) or halved quail (right).

Wild Game Substitution Charts

If there's a recipe you'd like to try, but you don't have the proper type of game, you can find a substitute in the charts on the following five pages. Just as chicken can replace turkey in many recipes, elk can replace venison, but the finished dish will have a different flavor than the original recipe. Full-flavored game like bear, raccoon or woodcock may overwhelm a delicate dish that calls for milder game.

If you have a species of game that is not listed in the charts, it can still be used as a substitute in suitable recipes, provided the cuts are the sizes called for. Again, remember that the flavors of the meats may vary.

Some domestic meats can be used in place of wild game, as noted in the individual categories. Generally, domestic meat has more fat and less flavor than wild game, but it is also more tender and will probably need less cooking time.

Big Game Substitution Chart

Although there are differences in taste, texture and fat content between the meats from hoofed big game species (deer, antelope, elk, moose and caribou), you can substitute one for another in a recipe, keeping in mind the tenderness of the specified cut and of the substitute. The substitution chart below is organized by species, starting with the largest — moose. Elk and caribou are similar to each other in size, and have been grouped together. Venison (deer) and antelope have also been grouped together.

Bear and wild boar are more similar to each other than to hoofed big game. However, *lean* bear, boar or javelina steak can be substituted for venison steak, and lean ground bear or boar can be substituted for ground venison. Any lean game meats are interchangeable in stew recipes. A recipe for venison roast needs to be adjusted slightly for use with bear, boar or javelina, since these roasts will probably have more fat. The bear or boar roast doesn't need added fat, and after the roast is cooked, you may want to skim the fat from the pan juices prior to making gravy.

One thing to keep in mind when cooking bear, boar or javelina is that the meat must be cooked to well done (165°F) because of the possibility of *trichinosis*. Thorough cooking destroys bacteria.

It's not as easy to substitute venison or other hoofed game for bear, boar or javelina in recipes, especially recipes for large cuts like roasts. Venison lacks internal marbling, so a recipe that works for a bear roast might produce a dry, tough roast if used with venison.

Domestic meats can be substituted for big game in recipes. Lean beef or buffalo works well for any recipe that calls for hoofed big game. Pork is an acceptable substitute for wild boar or javelina and can also be used in place of bear, although the color, flavor and texture are quite different.

Four ounces of uncooked big game meat (boneless weight) yields a cooked portion of approximately 3 ounces, which is the serving size recommended by the USDA.

SPECIES	CUT	SUBSTITUTE	COOKING METHOD
Moose *Tender*	Tenderloin (whole)	Tenderloin from elk or caribou Loin portion from moose, elk, caribou, venison or antelope	Oven roast, grill
	Loin (portion)	Loin portion from elk, caribou, venison or antelope Tenderloin from moose, elk or caribou	Oven roast, broil, grill, panbroil, panfry
	Loin steak	Loin steak from elk, caribou, venison or antelope Tenderloin from moose, elk, caribou, venison or antelope	Broil, grill, panbroil, panfry
	Loin chop	Loin chop from any big game animal	Broil, grill, panbroil, panfry
Intermediate tender	Rump roast	Rump roast from any big game animal Venison sirloin tip Rolled, tied bottom round from venison or antelope Eye of round from moose, elk or caribou	Oven roast, grill, braise
	Sirloin steak	Sirloin steak from any big game animal Loin chop from moose, elk, caribou, venison or antelope	Broil, grill, panbroil, panfry, stir-fry (strips)
	Round steak	Round steak from any big game animal Sirloin steak from any big game animal	Broil, grill, panbroil, panfry, stir-fry (strips)
Less tender	Boneless rolled shoulder roast	Boneless rolled shoulder roast from any big game animal Rolled rib roast from moose, elk or caribou Boneless chuck roast from moose, elk or caribou	Braise
	Bone-in chuck roast	Bone-in chuck roast from any big game animal Blade pot roast from moose, elk or caribou	Braise

Big Game Substitution Chart *(continued)*

SPECIES	CUT	SUBSTITUTE	COOKING METHOD
Elk or Caribou *Tender*	Tenderloin (whole)	Moose tenderloin Loin portion from moose, elk, caribou, venison or antelope	Oven roast, grill
	Loin (portion)	Loin portion from moose, venison or antelope Tenderloin from moose, elk, or caribou	Oven roast, broil, grill, panbroil, panfry
	Loin steak	Loin steak from moose, venison, or antelope Tenderloin from moose, elk, caribou, venison or antelope	Broil, grill, panbroil, panfry
	Loin chop	Loin chop from any big game animal	Broil, grill, panbroil, panfry
Intermediate tender	Rump roast	Rump roast from any big game animal Venison sirloin strip Rolled, tied bottom round from venison or antelope Eye of round from moose, elk or caribou	Oven roast, grill, braise
	Sirloin steak	Sirloin steak from any big game animal Loin chop from moose, elk, caribou, venison or antelope	Broil, grill, panbroil, panfry, stir-fry (strips)
	Round steak	Round steak from any big game animal Sirloin steak from any big game animal	Broil, grill, panbroil, panfry, stir-fry (strips)
Less tender	Boneless rolled shoulder roast	Boneless rolled shoulder roast from any big game animal Rolled rib roast from moose, elk or caribou Boneless chuck roast from moose, elk or caribou	Braise
	Bone-in chuck roast	Bone-in chuck roast from any big game animal Blade pot roast from moose, elk or caribou	Braise
Venison or Antelope *Tender*	Tenderloin (whole)	Tenderloin portion from moose, elk or caribou Loin portion from moose, elk, caribou, venison or antelope	Oven roast, grill
	Loin (portion)	Loin portion from moose, elk or caribou Tenderloin (whole) from moose, elk or caribou	Oven roast, broil, grill, panbroil, panfry
	Loin steak	Loin steak from moose, elk or caribou Tenderloin from moose, elk, caribou, venison or antelope	Broil, grill, panbroil, panfry
	Loin chop	Loin chop from any big game animal	Broil, grill, panbroil, panfry
Intermediate tender	Rump roast	Rump roast from any big game animal Venison sirloin tip Rolled, tied bottom round from venison or antelope Eye of round from moose, elk or caribou	Oven roast, grill, braise
	Round steak	Round steak from any big game animal Sirloin steak from any big game animal Loin chop from moose, elk, caribou, venison or antelope	Broil, grill, panbroil, panfry, stir-fry (strips)
Less tender	Boneless rolled shoulder roast	Boneless rolled shoulder roast from any big game animal Rolled rib roast from moose, elk or caribou Boneless chuck roast from moose, elk or caribou	Braise
	Bone-in chuck roast	Bone-in chuck roast from any big game animal Blade pot roast from moose, elk or caribou	Braise
Bear *Tender*	Loin chop	Loin chop from any big game animal	Broil, grill, panbroil, panfry
Intermediate tender	Rump roast	Rump roast from boar or javelina Rolled bottom round from venison or antelope with larding added during rolling	Oven roast, grill, braise
	Round steak	Round steak from any big game animal	Broil, grill, panbroil, panfry, braise

Big Game Substitution Chart *(continued)*

SPECIES	CUT	SUBSTITUTE	COOKING METHOD
Bear *Less tender*	Boneless rolled shoulder roast	Boneless rolled shoulder roast from any big game animal Rolled rib roast from moose, elk or caribou Boneless chuck roast from moose, elk or caribou	Braise
	Bone-in chuck roast	Bone-in chuck roast from any big game animal Blade pot roast from moose, elk or caribou	Braise
Boar or Javelina *Tender*	Loin	Loin portion from moose, elk, caribou, venison or antelope Tenderloin from moose, elk or caribou	Oven roast, grill
	Loin chop	Loin chop from any big game animal	Broil, grill, panbroil, panfry
Intermediate tender	Rump roast	Rump roast from bear Rolled bottom round from venison or antelope with larding added during rolling	Oven roast, grill, braise
	Round steak	Round steak from any big game animal	Broil, grill, panbroil, panfry, stir-fry (strips)
Less tender	Boneless rolled shoulder roast	Boneless rolled shoulder roast from any big game animal	Braise
	Bone-in chuck roast	Bone-in chuck roast from any big game animal Blade pot roast from moose, elk or caribou	Braise

Small Game Substitution Chart

Small game flavors range from rich, dark raccoon to delicate squirrel. Although you can substitute different species, remember that the final dish may taste quite different. Be particularly careful when substituting raccoon for rabbit or squirrel; its strong taste can overwhelm a mildly seasoned dish. Hare is tougher than rabbit or squirrel, and requires longer cooking.

Domestic rabbit will probably need less cooking time than wild rabbit.

If your recipe calls for a particular leftover or cooked small game, you can substitute any type of cooked small game, or even cooked pheasant, chicken or turkey. Cuts of fresh upland game birds can be easily substituted for small game cuts of similar size, as well.

SPECIES	APPROX. DRESSED WEIGHT	# OF SERVINGS	SUBSTITUTE	COOKING METHOD
Squirrel	¾ to 1 lb. (gray) 1 to 1½ lb. (fox)	1 1 to 1½	Cottontail rabbit (1 rabbit to 2 squirrels) Half of young snowshoe hare Portion of young raccoon Portion of domestic rabbit Pheasant or substitute (1 pheasant to 2 squirrels)	Panfry, bake, braise, stew, pressure-cook
Cottontail rabbit	1½ to 2 lbs.	2	2 squirrels Young snowshoe hare Portion of young raccoon Portion of domestic rabbit 1 pheasant or substitute	Panfry, bake, braise, stew, pressure-cook
Snowshoe hare	2½ to 3 lbs.	2 to 3	2 small cottontail rabbits 2 to 3 squirrels Half of young raccoon or portion of large raccoon Domestic rabbit	Braise, stew, pressure-cook
Raccoon	3 lbs. pieces	3 to 4	Snowshoe hare, quartered 2 cottontail rabbits, quartered 3 or 4 squirrels, quartered Domestic rabbit, cut into pieces	Braise, stew, stir-fry (strips)

Upland Game Birds Substitution Chart

As with small game, there are noticeable differences in meat color and flavor among upland game birds. The subtle berry flavor of a ruffed grouse, for example, may be overpowered in a recipe with strong flavors, just as strong-flavored sharptail may not work in a lightly seasoned dish. However, many recipes work well with any species.

Game-farm birds, such as pheasants, chukar partridge, quail and turkey, can be easily substituted for wild birds in recipes. A game-farm bird will probably have more fat than a wild one, so remove the excess before cooking. These birds are usually young, so they may not need as much cooking as wild ones.

You can substitute any type of cooked upland game bird for any other type. Cooked chicken or turkey breast or thighs are also good substitutes. Cuts of fresh small game species can also be substituted for upland game bird cuts of similar size.

SPECIES	APPROX. DRESSED WEIGHT	# OF SERVINGS	SUBSTITUTE	COOKING METHOD
Wild turkey (whole)	8 to 16 lbs.	5 to 10	Domestic turkey of similar weight (NOT prebasted type)	Oven roast
Wild turkey (any pieces)	3 to 4½ lbs.	6 to 8	2 pheasants, quartered 3 ruffed or sharptail grouse, halved 3 or 4 chukar or Hungarian partridge, halved 3 lbs. domestic turkey pieces, excess fat removed	Panfry, braise, bake
Pheasant (whole)	1½ to 2¼ lbs.	3 to 4	2 ruffed or sharptail grouse 2 chukar or Hungarian partridge	Oven roast, panbroil, panfry, braise, bake
2 pheasants (cut up)	3 to 4½ lbs.	6 to 8	Thighs and legs from wild turkey 3 or 4 ruffed or sharptail grouse, quartered 4 chukar or Hungarian partridge, quartered 8 quail, halved	Panfry, braise, bake
Pheasant (2 whole breasts, boneless)	1 lb.	4	Boned breast portion or thighs from turkey Boned breast and thighs from 2 ruffed or sharptail grouse, 2 chukar or Hungarian partridge Boned breasts from 4 quail Boned breasts from 6 or 7 doves	Panfry, deep-fry, grill, braise, bake
Ruffed or sharptail grouse* (whole)	1 to 1¼ lbs.	2 to 3	½ pheasant 1 chukar or Hungarian partridge	Oven roast, panfry, braise, grill, bake
Chukar or Hungarian partridge (whole)	¾ to 1 lb.	2	½ pheasant 1 ruffed or sharptail grouse	Oven roast, panfry, braise, bake
Quail	4 quail (4 to 6 oz. each)	4	1 pheasant, cut up 1½ ruffed or sharptail grouse, cut up 2 chukar or Hungarian partridge, quartered	Oven roast, panfry, braise, grill, bake
Woodcock	5 to 6 woodcock (5 oz. each)	4	1 pheasant, cut up 1½ ruffed grouse, cut up 2 chukar or Hungarian partridge, cut up 4 quail, halved	Panfry, braise, bake
Dove	6 or 7 doves (2 to 3 oz. each)	4	1 pheasant, cut up, breast sections halved 1½ ruffed or sharptail grouse, cut up, breast sections halved 2 chukar or Hungarian partridge, cut up, breast sections halved 4 quail, halved	Panfry, braise, bake

Note that while ruffed and sharptail grouse are similar in size, their meats differ greatly in color and flavor. Sharptail is much darker and stronger flavored.

Waterfowl Substitution Chart

With over 20 species of ducks and geese on this chart, we've taken a "mix-and-match" approach to substitutions. The chart is broken into four areas: Large Geese, Medium-size Geese, Small Geese/Large Ducks and Small Ducks. If the recipe calls for a Mallard, all you need do is locate it on the chart, then substitute any of the other ducks from that same area of the chart.

Breast meat from any of these birds can be substituted for mallard breast in recipes. Domestic ducks are generally too fatty to substitute for wild ducks. Upland game birds with dark meat also make good substitutes for duck if cuts are the same size.

If a recipe calls for a whole wild goose, you can substitute any wild goose of similar size. You can also substitute a domestic goose of the proper size, but the flavor is not as rich as wild goose. You will have to prick the skin of a domestic goose frequently during roasting to allow the excess fat to drain off; skim the fat from the pan juices prior to making gravy or sauce.

	SPECIES	APPROX. DRESSED WEIGHT	# OF SERVINGS	COOKING METHOD
Large Geese	**Giant Canada** Young Mature	4 to 6 lbs. 6½ to 10 lbs.	4 to 6 6 to 10	Oven roast, grill, panfry Parboil/roast, braise, stew
	Interior Canada Young Mature	3½ to 4½ lbs. 4¾ to 6 lbs.	4 to 5 5 to 10	Oven roast, grill, panfry Parboil/roast, braise, stew
Medium-size Geese	Lesser Canada	3 to 4½ lbs.	3 to 6	Oven roast, grill, panfry
	Snow or Blue Goose	3 to 4 lbs.	3 to 5	Oven roast, grill, panfry
	White-fronted Goose (Specklebelly)	3½ to 3¾ lbs.	3 to 5	Oven roast, grill, panfry
	Interior Canada Young	3½ to 4½ lbs.	4 to 5	Oven roast, grill, panfry
Small Geese/ Large Ducks	Cackling Canada	2 to 2½ lbs.	2 to 3	Oven roast, grill, panfry
	Brant	1¾ to 2½ lbs.	2 to 3	Oven roast, grill, panfry
	Canvasback	1¾ lbs.	2	Oven roast, grill, panfry
	Mallard	1¼ to 1½ lbs.	2	Oven roast, grill, panfry
	Black Duck	1¼ to 1½ lbs.	2	Oven roast, grill, panfry
	Redhead	1¼ lbs.	2	Oven roast, grill, panfry
	Greater Scaup (Bluebill)	1¼ lbs.	2	Oven roast, grill, panfry
Small Ducks	Goldeneye (Whistler)	1 to 1¼ lbs.	1 to 1½	Oven roast, grill, panfry
	Pintail	1 to 1¼ lbs.	1 to 1½	Oven roast, grill, panfry
	Gadwall	¾ to 1 lb.	1 to 1½	Oven roast, grill, panfry
	Lesser Scaup	¾ to 1 lb.	1 to 1½	Oven roast, grill, panfry
	Widgeon (Baldpate)	¾ to 1 lb.	1 to 1½	Oven roast, grill, panfry
	Ring-necked (Ringbill)	¾ lb.	1 to 1½	Oven roast, grill, panfry
	Wood Duck	½ to ¾ lb.	1	Oven roast, grill, panfry
	Bufflehead	5 oz. to ¾ lb.	1	Oven roast, grill, panfry
	Blue-winged Teal	½ lb.	1	Oven roast, grill, panfry
	Cinnamon Teal	5 oz. to ½ lb.	1	Oven roast, grill, panfry
	Green-winged Teal	5 to 6 oz.	1 or less	Oven roast, grill, panfry

Hot Pheasant Chunks ↑

Sally Shaffer – Circle CE Ranch, Dixon, South Dakota

¾ cup all-purpose flour
1½ teaspoons seasoned salt
¼ teaspoon pepper
1 lb. boneless skinless pheasant breast or substitute, cut into 1-inch pieces
¼ cup vegetable oil
½ cup margarine or butter, melted
2 tablespoons red pepper sauce

8 servings

In large plastic food-storage bag, combine flour, salt and pepper. Add pheasant pieces. Shake to coat.

In 12-inch nonstick skillet, heat oil over medium heat. Add pheasant pieces. Cook for 7 to 9 minutes, or until meat is golden brown, stirring frequently.

In small mixing bowl, combine margarine and red pepper sauce. Pour over pheasant pieces. Reduce heat to low. Cook for 25 to 30 minutes, or until meat is tender, stirring occasionally. Serve with additional red pepper sauce, if desired.

Per Serving: Calories: 281 • Protein: 15 g. • Carbohydrate: 9 g. • Fat: 20 g.
• Cholesterol: N/A • Sodium: 487 mg.
Exchanges: ⅔ starch, 1¾ medium-fat meat, 2¼ fat

Pheasant Breast Matches with Curry Dip

"Wonderful for a hot summer evening."
Louis Bignami – Moscow, Idaho

CURRY DIP:
¼ cup mayonnaise
¼ cup plain low-fat or nonfat yogurt
    or sour cream
¼ cup sliced green onions
2 teaspoons curry powder
½ teaspoon Worcestershire sauce
¼ teaspoon soy sauce

½ cup all-purpose flour
1 teaspoon salt

½ teaspoon pepper
1 lb. boneless skinless pheasant
    breast or substitute, cut into
    3 × 1-inch strips
3 eggs
1 cup unseasoned dry bread
    crumbs
⅓ cup ground walnuts
½ cup vegetable oil

8 servings

In small mixing bowl, combine dip ingredients. Cover with plastic wrap. Chill. In large plastic food-storage bag, combine flour, salt and pepper. Add pheasant strips. Shake to coat. In shallow dish, lightly beat eggs. On sheet of wax paper, combine bread crumbs and walnuts. Dip pheasant strips first in eggs and then dredge in bread crumb mixture to coat.

In 10-inch nonstick skillet, heat oil over medium heat. Add pheasant strips. Cook for 3 to 5 minutes, or until meat is golden brown, turning over once. Drain on paper-towel-lined plate. Serve with curry dip.

Per Serving: Calories: 366 • Protein: 20 g. • Carbohydrate: 18 g. • Fat: 24 g.
• Cholesterol: N/A • Sodium: 493 mg.
Exchanges: 1 starch, 2½ lean meat, 3¼ fat

Dove Breast Delight ↑

Ray Harper – Evansville, Indiana

4 wooden skewers (8-inch)
½ cup packed brown sugar
¼ cup margarine or butter
3 tablespoons white wine vinegar
10 boneless skinless whole dove
    breasts (1 to 2 oz. each), split
    in half
5 slices bacon, cut crosswise into
    quarters
1 can (8 oz.) whole water
    chestnuts, rinsed and drained

4 servings

Soak skewers in water for 30 minutes. Drain. Set aside. Prepare grill for barbecuing. Spray cooking grate with nonstick vegetable cooking spray. In 1-quart saucepan, combine sugar, margarine and vinegar. Cook over medium heat for 2 to 3 minutes, or until margarine is melted and sugar is dissolved, stirring constantly. Cover to keep warm. Set aside. Wrap each breast half with 1 bacon piece. Place 5 breast halves on each skewer, alternating with water chestnuts. Set aside.

Arrange kabobs on prepared grate. Grill, covered, for 10 to 15 minutes, or until bacon is brown and crisp and meat is no longer pink, turning kabobs over several times during grilling. Place kabobs in shallow dish. Pour margarine mixture over kabobs. Remove kabobs from margarine mixture just before serving.

Nutritional information not available.

Turkey Tracks

"We have a lot of wild turkey and this is a good way to use it."
Ruth E. Taggart – Dallas, South Dakota

PASTRY:

- 1 pkg. (8 oz.) cream cheese, softened
- 1 cup margarine or butter, softened
- 2 cups all-purpose flour

FILLING:

- 3½ cups cubed cooked wild turkey or substitute (about 1 lb.), ¼-inch cubes
- ⅓ cup shredded pasteurized process cheese loaf
- ⅓ cup thinly sliced celery
- ⅓ cup mayonnaise or salad dressing
- 2 tablespoons sliced green onion
- 2 tablespoons sour cream
- ¼ teaspoon salt
- ¼ teaspoon pepper

16 servings

Heat oven to 400°F. In medium mixing bowl, cut cream cheese and margarine into flour until soft dough forms. Cover with plastic wrap. Chill 1 hour.

Shape dough into 48 balls, about 1 inch in diameter. Press each ball into bottom and up sides of un-greased 1¾-inch muffin cups. Bake for 8 to 10 minutes, or until golden brown.

In large mixing bowl, combine all filling ingredients. Spoon about 1 tablespoon turkey mixture into each pastry shell. Bake for 3 to 5 minutes, or until cheese is melted.

Per Serving: Calories: 310 • Protein: 13 g. • Carbohydrate: 13 g. • Fat: 23 g. • Cholesterol: 46 mg. • Sodium: 333 mg. Exchanges: ¾ starch, 1½ medium-fat meat, 3 fat

Pheasant Supreme

Raymond E. Steinbis – Sycamore, Illinois

- ½ cup all-purpose flour
- ½ teaspoon salt
- ¼ teaspoon pepper
- ¾ to 1 lb. boneless skinless pheasant breast and thigh or substitute, cut into 3 × 1-inch strips
- 2 eggs
- 3 tablespoons Dijon mustard
- ½ cup unseasoned dry bread crumbs
- 3 tablespoons olive oil

6 to 8 servings

In large plastic food-storage bag, combine flour, salt and pepper. Add pheasant strips. Shake to coat. In shallow dish, lightly beat eggs and mustard. Place bread crumbs on sheet of wax paper. Dip pheasant strips first in egg mixture and then dredge in bread crumbs to coat.

In 10-inch nonstick skillet, heat oil over medium heat. Add pheasant strips. Cook for 3 to 5 minutes, or until meat is golden brown, turning over once. Serve with sweet and sour sauce, barbecue sauce or honey-mustard sauce, if desired.

Per Serving: Calories: 192 • Protein: 15 g. • Carbohydrate: 12 g. • Fat: 9 g. • Cholesterol: 99 mg. • Sodium: 398 mg.
Exchanges: ⅔ starch, 2 lean meat, ½ fat

Sprig Spring Rolls

"Really stretches duck as an appetizer or entrée. Good choice for badly shot-up birds."
    Louis Bignami – Moscow, Idaho

1 dressed wild duck (1½ to 2¼ lbs.), cut up, skin on	½ teaspoon grated fresh gingerroot
8 cups water	1 tablespoon cornstarch
1 cup sliced celery	1 tablespoon dry sherry
1 bay leaf	1 tablespoon soy sauce
6 peppercorns	1 tablespoon sesame oil
2 cups shredded green cabbage	14 to 16 eggroll skins (7-inch square)
½ cup canned sliced water chestnuts, drained and chopped	1 egg yolk mixed with 1 teaspoon water
¼ cup shredded carrot	4 cups vegetable oil
2 tablespoons chopped shallots	

14 to 16 servings

In 6-quart Dutch oven or stockpot, combine duck pieces, water, celery, bay leaf and peppercorns. Bring to a boil over medium-high heat. Reduce heat to medium. Cook for 20 to 25 minutes, or until meat is tender. Remove duck pieces from broth. Cool slightly. Shred meat. Discard bones and skin. Strain broth and freeze for future use.

In large mixing bowl, combine shredded meat, cabbage, water chestnuts, carrot, shallots, gingerroot, cornstarch, sherry, soy sauce and sesame oil. Follow photo tip at right for rolling spring rolls.

In wok or 12-inch nonstick skillet, heat oil over medium-high heat. Add spring rolls. Cook, 3 or 4 at a time, for 3 to 4 minutes, or until golden brown, turning over once. Drain on paper-towel-lined plate. Serve spring rolls with plum sauce, sweet and sour sauce or hot mustard, if desired.

PLACE 2 heaping tablespoons duck mixture just below center of each egg-roll skin. Roll up, folding in sides. Brush top corner with egg yolk mixture; continue rolling to complete seal.

Per Serving: Calories: 190 • Protein: 8 g.
• Carbohydrate: 21 g. • Fat: 8 g.
• Cholesterol: 32 mg. • Sodium: 262 mg.
Exchanges: 1 starch, ¾ lean meat,
1 vegetable, 1 fat

19

Korean Duck Kabobs

Joan N. Cone – Williamburg, Virginia

- 1 cup vegetable oil
- 1 small onion, cut into chunks
- ⅔ cup sugar
- ¼ cup plus 2 tablespoons soy sauce
- 1 tablespoon all-purpose flour
- 1 clove garlic
- 2 tablespoons sesame seed, toasted
- ¾ to 1 lb. boneless skinless wild duck breast or substitute, cut into 1-inch pieces (36 pieces)
- 12 wooden skewers (6-inch)
- 1 can (8 oz.) pineapple chunks in juice, drained
- 6 green onions, cut into 1½-inch lengths (24 lengths)

4 to 6 servings

In food processor or blender, combine oil, onion, sugar, soy sauce, flour and garlic. Process until smooth. Pour marinade into medium mixing bowl. Stir in sesame seed. Reserve ½ cup marinade. Cover with plastic wrap. Chill. Add duck pieces to remaining marinade. Stir to coat. Cover with plastic wrap. Refrigerate 8 hours or overnight.

Soak skewers in water for 30 minutes. Drain. Drain and discard marinade from duck pieces. On each skewer, alternate 3 duck pieces with 1 or 2 pineapple chunks and 2 green onion lengths. Arrange kabobs on rack in broiler pan. Place under broiler with surface of meat 3 to 4 inches from heat. Broil for 4 to 6 minutes, or until meat is desired doneness, turning kabobs over once and brushing with reserved marinade several times.

Per Serving: Calories: 334 • Protein: 14 g.
• Carbohydrate: 20 g. • Fat: 22 g.
• Cholesterol: N/A • Sodium: 556 mg.
Exchanges: 2 lean meat, 1⅓ fruit, 3 fat

Sausage-stuffed Mushrooms →

Bill Stevens – Fridley, Minnesota

42 fresh medium mushrooms
   (about 1½ lbs.)
½ lb. bulk venison sausage or
   substitute, crumbled
¾ cup shredded mozzarella cheese
¼ cup unseasoned dry bread
   crumbs
2 tablespoons snipped fresh parsley

14 servings

Heat oven to 450°F. Remove stems
from mushroom caps. Set caps
aside. Finely chop stems.

In 10-inch nonstick skillet, combine chopped stems and sausage.
Cook over medium heat for 5 to 7
minutes, or until meat is no longer
pink, stirring frequently. Remove
from heat. Stir in cheese, bread
crumbs and parsley.

Arrange mushroom caps stem-side-
up on 15½ × 10½-inch jelly roll
pan. Spoon about 1 tablespoon
sausage mixture into each cap.
Bake for 6 to 8 minutes, or until
cheese is melted.

Per Serving: Calories: 79 • Protein: 5 g.
• Carbohydrate: 4 g. • Fat: 5 g.
• Cholesterol: 19 mg. • Sodium: 156 mg.
Exchanges: ½ medium-fat meat,
½ vegetable, ½ fat

Wyoming Wontons ↑

"Any type of game can be used, although antelope is particularly suited to this recipe."
Teresa Marrone – Minneapolis, Minnesota

1 teaspoon vegetable oil
½ lb. lean ground antelope or
   substitute, crumbled
½ cup finely chopped onion
3 tablespoons thick and chunky
   salsa
2 cloves garlic, minced
1 teaspoon dried sage leaves,
   crumbled
½ teaspoon ground cumin
½ teaspoon salt
1 can (4 oz.) peeled whole green
   chilies, drained
30 wonton skins
1¼ cups shredded Monterey Jack
   cheese
   Vegetable oil

10 servings

Heat oven to 200°F. In 10-inch nonstick skillet, heat 1 teaspoon oil over
medium heat. Add ground antelope. Cook for 8 to 10 minutes, or until
meat is no longer pink, stirring occasionally. Add onion, salsa, garlic,
sage, cumin and salt. Cook for 5 minutes, stirring occasionally. Remove
from heat. Cover to keep warm. Set filling aside.

Cut chilies to yield 30 pieces. Place 1 piece chili in center of 1 wonton
skin. Top with heaping teaspoon filling and heaping teaspoon cheese.
Moisten edges of wonton skin with water. Fold wonton skin diagonally
over filling, pressing edges to seal. Moisten 1 corner of wonton. Bring 2
corners together and overlap. Press together to seal. Repeat with remaining chili pieces, wonton skins, filling and cheese.

In deep-fat fryer, heat 3 inches vegetable oil to 400°F. Cook wontons, 3 at
a time, for 1½ to 2 minutes, or until deep golden brown, turning over once.
Drain on paper-towel-lined plate. Place in oven to keep warm. Serve with
additional thick and chunky salsa or blue cheese dressing, if desired.

Per Serving: Calories: 242 • Protein: 10 g. • Carbohydrate: 16 g. • Fat: 15 g.
• Cholesterol: 39 mg. • Sodium: 429 mg.
Exchanges: 1 starch, 1¼ medium-fat meat, 1¾ fat

21

Microwave Venison Chip Dip

Vicki J. Snyder – Columbus, Ohio

½ lb. lean ground venison or substitute, crumbled
1 - lb. pasteurized process cheese loaf with jalapeño peppers, cut into 1-inch cubes
1 cup chopped seeded tomato, divided
1 can (4 oz.) chopped green chilies, drained
¼ cup sliced black olives
¼ teaspoon ground cumin
¼ teaspoon garlic powder
¼ cup sliced green onions

3 cups, 12 servings

In 2-quart casserole, microwave ground venison on High for 2 to 4 minutes, or until meat is no longer pink, stirring once to break apart. Drain. Add cheese, ¾ cup tomato and the remaining ingredients, except green onions. Mix well.

Microwave on High for 4 to 6 minutes, or until mixture is hot and cheese is melted, stirring once. Garnish dip with remaining ¼ cup chopped tomato and the sliced green onions. Serve with tortilla chips or use as a potato topper, if desired.

Per Serving: Calories: 166 • Protein: 10 g.
• Carbohydrate: 6 g. • Fat: 12 g.
• Cholesterol: 44 mg. • Sodium: 679 mg.
Exchanges: 1¼ medium-fat meat, 1 vegetable, 1¼ fat

Country Pâté à la Potts ↑

Jim Potts – Lewes, Delaware

1 cup brandy
1 teaspoon ground ginger
½ teaspoon ground nutmeg
½ teaspoon ground allspice
¼ teaspoon ground mace
¼ cup butter
3 cups coarsely chopped onions
1 bulb garlic, peeled and minced (16 to 18 cloves)
1 lb. lean ground venison or substitute, crumbled

1 lb. lean ground pork, crumbled
1 lb. lean ground veal, crumbled
1 lb. fresh pork back fat, cut into 1-inch strips
8 oz. fresh pork liver, cut into 1-inch strips
3 eggs, beaten
1 tablespoon salt
1 teaspoon freshly ground pepper
1 teaspoon dried parsley flakes
1 teaspoon dried basil leaves

1 lb. sliced bacon
2 bay leaves

Two loaves, 16 servings per loaf

Follow directions on opposite page.

Per Serving: Calories: 341 • Protein: 11 g.
• Carbohydrate: 2 g. • Fat: 31 g.
• Cholesterol: 193 mg. • Sodium: 356 mg.
Exchanges: 1½ high-fat meat, ½ vegetable, 3¾ fat

How to Make Country Pâté à la Potts

COMBINE brandy, ginger, nutmeg, allspice and mace in 1-quart saucepan. Cook over medium-high heat for 3 to 5 minutes, or until hot. Reduce heat to medium-low. Simmer for 20 to 25 minutes, or until mixture is reduced by half. Remove from heat. Cool completely. Set aside.

MELT butter in 10-inch nonstick skillet over medium heat. Add onions and garlic. Cook for 4 to 5 minutes, or until onions are tender, stirring occasionally. Cool completely. Set aside.

COMBINE ¼ lb. of each of the following in large food processor: ground venison, ground pork, ground veal and pork back fat. Add 2 oz. of pork liver. Process mixture until smooth. Transfer to large mixing bowl. Repeat with remaining ground meats, back fat and liver. Add brandy and onion mixtures to meat mixture. Mix well. Cover with plastic wrap. Refrigerate 24 hours.

HEAT oven to 325°F. Add eggs, salt, pepper, parsley and basil to meat mixture. Mix well. Reserve 4 slices bacon. Line bottom and sides of two 8 × 5-inch glass loaf dishes with remaining bacon, cutting strips to fit. Fill prepared dishes evenly with meat mixture. Top each with bay leaf. Cover evenly with reserved bacon. Cover each dish tightly with heavy-duty foil, allowing about 1½-inch overhang on each side.

PLACE loaf dishes in 13 × 9-inch baking dish. Pour water into baking dish to depth of 1 inch. Place in oven. Bake for 3 hours. Remove loaf dishes from baking dish. Cool loaves for 1 hour. Place foil-wrapped brick on each foil-covered loaf. Refrigerate, weighted, for 8 to 12 hours.

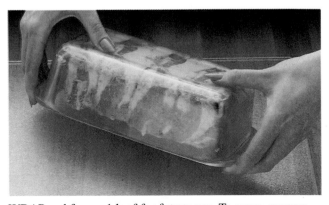

WRAP and freeze 1 loaf for future use. To serve, remove foil. Loosen edges and remove pâté from dish. Remove and discard bacon and bay leaf. Cut slices and serve on French bread or crackers garnished with tiny dill pickles (cornichons), or use as sandwich meat, if desired.

Main Dishes

Big Game

← Roast Moose with Orange-Lingonberry Sauce

Teresa Marrone – Minneapolis, Minnesota

MARINADE:

    2 medium onions, sliced
    1 cup orange juice
  ½ cup olive oil
    2 tablespoons lemon juice
    1 large clove garlic, minced
    1 teaspoon dried marjoram leaves
  ¼ teaspoon ground ginger

  3-lb. boneless moose round or rump roast or
       substitute, well trimmed
2¾ cups game broth or beef broth, divided
  ½ cup drained lingonberries
    1 teaspoon grated orange peel
  ¼ to ½ teaspoon bouquet sauce
    2 tablespoons margarine or butter, softened

12 servings

In large nonmetallic bowl, combine marinade ingredients. Add roast. Turn to coat. Cover with plastic wrap. Refrigerate 24 hours, turning roast over occasionally. Remove roast from marinade. Pat dry. Strain and reserve marinade.

Heat oven to 350°F. Place roast in bottom of 3-quart roasting pan. Add ¾ cup broth. Insert meat thermometer in roast. Bake for 1½ to 1¾ hours for rare (135°F) to medium (155°F), or until meat is desired doneness, basting roast frequently with pan juices (add more broth if needed). Let roast stand, tented with foil, for 10 minutes. (Internal temperature will rise 5°F during standing.)

Meanwhile, in 2-quart saucepan, combine reserved marinade with remaining 2 cups broth. Bring to a boil over high heat. Reduce heat to medium. Cook for 30 to 35 minutes, or until mixture is reduced by half, stirring frequently. Add lingonberries, peel and bouquet sauce. Cook for 1 to 2 minutes, or until sauce is hot and bubbly. Reduce heat to low. Stir in margarine, 1 teaspoon at a time, until well blended. Carve roast across grain into thin slices. Serve sauce with roast.

Per Serving: Calories: 241 • Protein: 26 g. • Carbohydrate: 6 g.
• Fat: 12 g. • Cholesterol: 67 mg. • Sodium: 288 mg.
Exchanges: 3¾ lean meat, ⅓ fruit

Elk Camp Roast

William F. Carney – Beverly, Massachusetts

  ¾ cup margarine or butter
    1 medium onion, thinly sliced
    1 cup thinly sliced carrots
  ½ cup thinly sliced celery
    3 to 4-lb. boneless elk rump roast or substitute
    2 cinnamon sticks, cut in half
1½ cups port wine
  ¼ cup bourbon
    2 slices bacon, cut in half crosswise
  ½ teaspoon ground allspice

14 servings

Heat oven to 450°F. In 10-inch nonstick skillet, melt margarine over medium heat. Add onion, carrots and celery. Cook for 2 to 3 minutes, or until vegetables are tender-crisp, stirring occasionally. Spoon evenly into bottom of 3-quart roasting pan. Place roast on top of vegetables. Add cinnamon sticks. Pour wine and bourbon around roast. Arrange bacon slices across roast.

Insert meat thermometer in roast. Bake for 10 minutes. Reduce heat to 350°F. Bake for 1 to 1½ hours for medium-rare (145°F) to medium (155°F), or until meat is desired doneness, basting roast frequently with pan juices. Let roast stand, tented with foil, for 10 minutes. (Internal temperature will rise 5°F during standing.) Carve roast across grain into thin slices.

Skim and discard fat from juices in pan. Place juices in 1-quart saucepan. Simmer over medium heat for 15 to 20 minutes, or until sauce is reduced by one-fourth. Stir in allspice. Serve sauce with roast.

Per Serving: Calories: 253 • Protein: 27 g. • Carbohydrate: 5 g.
• Fat: 13 g. • Cholesterol: 65 mg. • Sodium: 212 mg.
Exchanges: 3½ lean meat, 1 vegetable, ¾ fat

Cadiz Township Venison Roast

"This is a simple, easy way to prepare a roast. It reminds me of the hills, woodlots and deer of this southern Wisconsin township I've hunted and loved for many years."
   Thomas Carpenter – Maple Grove, Minnesota

1   large onion, thinly sliced
3   to 4-lb. boneless rolled tied
       venison shoulder roast or
       substitute
1   teaspoon freshly ground pepper
1   clove garlic, minced
¼   to ½ lb. side pork, sliced
       (¼-inch slices)
1   cup dry red wine

                        14 servings

Heat oven to 350°F. Place onion in bottom of 3-quart roasting pan with cover. Place roast on top of onion. Sprinkle roast with pepper and garlic. Arrange side pork slices across roast. Pour wine over roast. Cover tightly.

Bake for 2 to 2½ hours, or until meat is tender. Remove cover. Bake for 30 minutes longer. Let roast stand for 10 minutes.

Remove and discard side pork slices. Carve roast across grain into thin slices. Skim and discard fat from juices in pan. Serve roast with cooked onion and pan juices.

Per Serving: Calories: 205 • Protein: 28 g. • Carbohydrate: 2 g. • Fat: 9 g.
• Cholesterol: 106 mg. • Sodium: 63 mg.
Exchanges: 3¾ lean meat, ¼ vegetable

Slow-lane Venison

"Cook this in the oven, a crock pot, or a covered roaster in campfire coals. The secret is long, slow roasting at low temperatures."

Janet Groene – DeLand, Florida

- 3 to 4-lb. boneless venison rump roast or substitute
- 3 slices bacon, cut in half crosswise
- 1 can (8 oz.) tomato sauce
- ½ cup catsup
- ½ cup chopped onion
- 2 tablespoons packed brown sugar
- 2 tablespoons Worcestershire sauce
- 2 tablespoons cider vinegar
- ½ teaspoon garlic powder
- ½ teaspoon coarsely ground pepper

14 servings

Heat oven to 325°F. Place roast in bottom of 3-quart roasting pan with cover. Arrange bacon slices across roast. In medium mixing bowl, combine remaining ingredients. Pour mixture over roast. Cover tightly.

Bake for 2 to 3 hours, or until meat is tender. Let roast stand for 10 minutes. Carve roast across grain into thin slices, or shred. Serve in buttered hamburger buns with coleslaw and chilled cranberry sauce, if desired.

Per Serving: Calories: 190 • Protein: 27 g. • Carbohydrate: 7 g. • Fat: 6 g. • Cholesterol: 100 mg. • Sodium: 315 mg. Exchanges: 3 medium-fat meat, 1¼ vegetable

Peppery Southwestern-style Venison Roast ↑

Col. Lyle B. Otto – Gig Harbor, Washington

- 3 to 4-lb. boneless venison rump roast or substitute
- ½ cup catsup
- ¼ cup packed brown sugar
- 1 tablespoon prepared mustard
- 1 tablespoon liquid smoke flavoring (optional)
- 1 tablespoon fresh lemon juice
- 1 tablespoon soy sauce
- 2 teaspoons Worcestershire sauce
- 2 teaspoons celery salt
- 2 teaspoons coarsely ground pepper
- 1 teaspoon garlic powder
- 1 teaspoon onion powder
- ¼ teaspoon crushed red pepper flakes
  Dash ground nutmeg

14 servings

Heat oven to 350°F. Place roast in bottom of 3-quart roasting pan with cover. Set aside. In medium mixing bowl, combine remaining ingredients. Pour mixture over roast. Cover tightly. Bake for 2 to 2½ hours, or until meat is tender. Remove cover. Bake for 30 minutes longer. Let roast stand for 10 minutes. Carve roast across grain into thin slices.

Per Serving: Calories: 164 • Protein: 26 g. • Carbohydrate: 7 g. • Fat: 3 g. • Cholesterol: 96 mg. • Sodium: 348 mg. Exchanges: 3 lean meat, 1 vegetable

Spiced Bear Roast

Thomas K. Squier – Aberdeen, North Carolina

3½ to 4-lb. boneless bear rump roast or substitute,
    well trimmed
12 whole cloves
1½ cups thinly sliced carrots
1½ cups thinly sliced celery
  1 cup chopped onions
  1 cup dry red wine
 ¾ cup water
 ¼ cup margarine or butter, melted
  2 teaspoons cayenne
  1 teaspoon ground allspice
 ½ teaspoon pepper
  2 slices bacon, cut in half crosswise

14 to 16 servings

Heat oven to 400°F. Place roast in bottom of 3-quart roasting pan with cover. With sharp knife, cut 12 slits, ½ inch deep, in top of roast. Place 1 clove in each slit.

In medium mixing bowl, combine remaining ingredients, except bacon. Pour mixture over roast. Arrange bacon slices across roast. Insert meat thermometer in roast. Cover tightly. Bake for 20 minutes.

Reduce heat to 325°F. Bake for 2 to 2½ hours, or until meat is tender and internal temperature registers 165°F. Remove cover. Bake for 15 minutes longer. Let roast stand for 10 minutes. Carve roast across grain into thin slices.

Per Serving: Calories: 225 • Protein: 22 g. • Carbohydrate: 3 g.
• Fat: 13 g. • Cholesterol: N/A • Sodium: N/A
Exchanges: 3 lean meat, ⅔ vegetable, 1 fat

Marinated Garlic Bear Roast

Keith Sutton – Benton, Arkansas

MARINADE:

- 1 cup chopped onions
- ⅓ cup vegetable oil
- ⅓ cup soy sauce
- 1 teaspoon chili powder
- 1 teaspoon garlic powder
- 1 teaspoon ground ginger

- 3½ to 4-lb. boneless bear leg roast or substitute, well trimmed
- 8 cloves garlic
- ½ teaspoon freshly ground pepper
- ⅛ teaspoon salt
- 1 can (6 oz.) sliced mushrooms, drained

14 to 16 servings

In 3-quart enamel-coated roasting pan with cover, combine marinade ingredients. With sharp knife, cut 8 slits, 2 inches deep, in top of roast. Place 1 clove garlic in each slit. Place roast in pan, turning to coat with marinade. Sprinkle roast with pepper and salt. Cover tightly. Refrigerate 12 to 24 hours, turning roast over once.

Heat oven to 325°F. Insert meat thermometer in roast. Re-cover. Bake for 2 to 2½ hours, or until meat is tender and internal temperature registers 165°F, adding mushrooms during last 15 minutes. Let roast stand for 10 minutes. Carve roast across grain into thin slices. Skim and discard fat from juices in pan. Serve roast with pan juices.

Per Serving: Calories: 213 • Protein: 22 g.
• Carbohydrate: 2 g. • Fat: 12 g.
• Cholesterol: N/A • Sodium: N/A
Exchanges: 3 lean meat, ½ vegetable, ¾ fat

Venison Bombers ↑

Teresa Marrone – Minneapolis, Minnesota

- 3-lb. boneless venison rump roast or substitute
- 6 cups venison broth or beef broth
- 2 medium red or green peppers, cut into 2 × ½-inch strips
- 2 medium onions, cut into ¾-inch wedges
- 1 bulb garlic, separated into cloves, peeled and sliced
- 2 dried hot peppers, crumbled, seeds removed (optional)
- 2 teaspoons dried oregano leaves

- 1½ teaspoons dried rosemary leaves
- 1½ teaspoons dried thyme leaves
- 1½ teaspoons pepper
- 12 hard rolls, split
- 1½ cups shredded lettuce
- 12 slices (1.2 oz. each) Provolone cheese
- 24 pepperoncini peppers, stems removed, cut into strips (optional)
- 4 medium tomatoes, thinly sliced

12 servings

In 6-quart ovenproof Dutch oven or stockpot, combine roast, broth, red or green pepper strips, onions, garlic, dried peppers, oregano, rosemary, thyme and pepper. Bring to a boil over medium-high heat. Reduce heat to low. Cover. Cook for 2½ to 3½ hours, or until meat is tender.

Remove meat from broth. Cool slightly. Carve roast across grain into thin slices. Return slices to broth. Cook over medium-low heat for 10 to 15 minutes, or until hot.

Heat oven to 350°F. Scoop out about half of inside portion of each roll to make a well. (Reserve scooped-out bread for future use.) Place tops and bottoms of rolls together and arrange on baking sheet. Bake for 5 to 8 minutes, or until hot. Spoon about ½ cup sliced meat mixture into bottom half of each roll. Spoon some of broth over meat. Top with lettuce, cheese, pepperoncini peppers and tomatoes. Place tops of rolls over cheese. Serve with additional broth for dipping, if desired.

Per Serving: Calories: 469 • Protein: 43 g. • Carbohydrate: 39 g. • Fat: 15 g.
• Cholesterol: 120 mg. • Sodium: 1085 mg.
Exchanges: 2 starch, 4¾ lean meat, 2 vegetable

Jay "D" Flattum – Lofton Ridge Deer Farm, Chisago City, Minnesota

3	tablespoons margarine or butter
2	medium onions, thinly sliced
1	medium green pepper, thinly sliced
1	medium red pepper, thinly sliced
½	teaspoon garlic salt
¼	teaspoon pepper
⅛	teaspoon cayenne
4	boneless venison loin steaks or substitute (4 oz. each), pounded to ¼-inch thickness
1	cup shredded mozzarella cheese
2	tablespoons grated Parmesan cheese
4	kaiser or sourdough rolls

4 servings

In 12-inch nonstick skillet, melt margarine over medium heat. Add onions, green and red peppers, garlic salt, pepper and cayenne. Cook for 3 to 5 minutes, or until vegetables are tender-crisp, stirring frequently. Remove vegetable mixture from skillet. Cover to keep warm. Set aside.

In same skillet, cook steaks over medium heat for 4 to 6 minutes, or until meat is desired doneness, turning steaks over once. Spoon vegetable mixture over steaks. Sprinkle evenly with mozzarella and Parmesan cheeses. Reduce heat to low. Cover. Cook for 3 to 5 minutes, or until mozzarella is melted. Serve steaks, topped with vegetables and cheese, in rolls.

Per Serving: Calories: 513 • Protein: 40 g. • Carbohydrate: 41 g. • Fat: 21 g. • Cholesterol: 120 mg. • Sodium: 803 mg. Exchanges: 2 starch, 4 lean meat, 2 vegetable, 1¾ fat

Venison au Poivre

Brian DeCicco and Barbara Canton – Affairs to Remember Catering, Pawling, New York

1¼	teaspoons salt, divided	¼	cup all-purpose flour
4	boneless venison round or loin steaks or substitute (4 oz. each), ½ inch thick	2	tablespoons vegetable oil
		¼	cup brandy
		½	cup whipping cream
2	teaspoons coarsely ground pepper	1	tablespoon assorted whole peppercorns

4 servings

Sprinkle steaks evenly with 1 teaspoon salt. Press pepper evenly into both sides of steaks. Dredge steaks in flour to coat.

In 10-inch nonstick skillet, heat oil over medium heat. Add steaks. Cook for 6 to 8 minutes, or until meat is desired doneness, turning steaks over once. Transfer steaks to warm platter. Cover to keep warm. Set aside.

Drain and discard oil from skillet. Add brandy to skillet. Stir to loosen browned bits in skillet (flame brandy, if desired).

Add remaining ¼ teaspoon salt, the cream and peppercorns. Cook over medium heat for 3 to 4 minutes, or until sauce is reduced and slightly thickened. Spoon sauce over steaks.

Per Serving: Calories: 371 • Protein: 28 g. • Carbohydrate: 9 g. • Fat: 21 g. • Cholesterol: 137 mg. • Sodium: 756 mg. Exchanges: ½ starch, 3¾ lean meat, 2 fat

Wild Boar & Kraut Casserole →

"This one survives in a low oven until the most tardy hunters arrive."
Louis Bignami – Moscow, Idaho

- 2 tablespoons vegetable oil
- 6 bone-in boar chops or substitute (4 oz. each), ¾ to 1 inch thick
- 1 jar (2 lbs.) sauerkraut, rinsed and well drained
- 1 to 1½ lbs. smoked Polish sausage links (about 6)
- 4 cloves garlic, minced
- 14 juniper berries
- 1 teaspoon pepper
- ½ teaspoon salt
- 1 bay leaf
- 2⅓ cups dark beer
- 1½ cups shredded peeled potatoes
- 1 medium red cooking apple, cored and cut into 1-inch chunks
- 1 medium yellow cooking apple, cored and cut into 1-inch chunks
- 1 medium green cooking apple, cored and cut into 1-inch chunks

6 servings

Heat oven to 350°F. In 6-quart oven-proof Dutch oven or stockpot, heat oil over medium-high heat. Add boar chops. Cook for 5 to 7 minutes, or just until meat is browned on both sides. Remove from heat. Remove chops from pan. Set aside.

Into same Dutch oven, spoon half of sauerkraut. Top with chops and sausages. In medium mixing bowl, combine remaining sauerkraut, the garlic, berries, pepper, salt and bay leaf. Spoon mixture over chops and sausage. Pour beer over mixture. Cover. Bake for 1 hour.

Stir in potatoes and apples. Re-cover. Bake for 30 to 45 minutes, or until apples are tender. Remove and discard bay leaf. Serve with thick slices of crusty bread, if desired.

Per Serving: Calories: 576 • Protein: 39 g. • Carbohydrate: 27 g. • Fat: 34 g. • Cholesterol: N/A • Sodium: N/A Exchanges: ½ starch, 4¾ medium-fat meat, 1¾ vegetable, ⅔ fruit, 2 fat

Hoppin' John Wild Hog Chops

"This is a traditional New Year's dish!" Thomas K. Squier – Aberdeen, North Carolina

- 5 slices bacon, cut into ½-inch pieces
- 8 bone-in boar chops or substitute (4 oz. each), ¾ to 1 inch thick
- ½ cup chopped onion
- 1 clove garlic, minced
- 2 cans (15 oz. each) black-eyed peas, rinsed and drained
- 2 jars (12 oz. each) mushroom gravy
- ½ teaspoon salt
- ½ teaspoon pepper
- 1 cup hot cooked white rice
- 8 green pepper slices

4 servings

In 12-inch nonstick skillet, cook bacon over medium heat until brown and crisp. With slotted spoon, remove bacon from skillet. Drain on paper-towel-lined plate. Set aside.

To same skillet, add chops, onion and garlic. Cook over medium heat for 5 to 7 minutes, or just until meat is browned on both sides. Add peas, gravy, salt and pepper. Bring to a boil over medium-high heat. Reduce heat to low. Cover. Simmer for 30 minutes.

Add rice. Simmer for 35 to 45 minutes, or until meat is tender, stirring occasionally. Garnish with bacon and pepper slices.

Per Serving: Calories: 641 • Protein: 42 g. • Carbohydrate: 59 g. • Fat: 26 g. • Cholesterol: N/A • Sodium: N/A Exchanges: 3¾ starch, 4 lean meat, ½ vegetable, 2½ fat

Java-Schnitz

Bob Schranck – Golden Valley, Minnesota

⅓ cup all-purpose flour
½ teaspoon salt
¼ teaspoon pepper
8 javelina loin steaks (2 to 3 oz. each), pounded to ¼-inch thickness
2 eggs, beaten
½ cup unseasoned dry bread crumbs
3 tablespoons vegetable oil
½ cup butter
¼ cup snipped fresh parsley
4 to 8 lemon wedges

4 servings

In shallow dish, combine flour, salt and pepper. Dredge steaks in flour mixture to coat. Dip floured steaks first in eggs and then dredge in bread crumbs to coat.

In 12-inch nonstick skillet, heat oil over medium heat. Add steaks. Cook for 5 to 7 minutes, or until meat is well done, turning steaks over once. Transfer steaks to warm platter. Cover to keep warm. Set aside. Wipe out skillet with paper towels.

In same skillet, melt butter over medium-low heat. Cook for 1 to 2 minutes longer, or until lightly browned. Sprinkle parsley over steaks. Pour browned butter over steaks. Serve with lemon wedges.

Nutritional information not available.

Javelina Loin

Bob Hirsch – Cave Creek, Arizona

4 javelina loin steaks (2 to 3 oz. each), ½ inch thick
¼ teaspoon salt
¼ teaspoon pepper
3 tablespoons margarine or butter
⅓ cup pine nuts
4 oz. fresh mushrooms, thinly sliced (1½ cups)
2 cloves garlic, minced
¼ cup Burgundy wine

2 to 3 servings

Sprinkle steaks with salt and pepper. Set aside. In 10-inch nonstick skillet, melt margarine over medium-low heat. Add pine nuts. Cook for 2 to 3 minutes, or until golden brown, stirring frequently. With slotted spoon, transfer pine nuts to small mixing bowl. Set aside.

To same skillet, add mushrooms and garlic. Cook over medium-low heat for 2 to 3 minutes, or until tender, stirring frequently. With slotted spoon, remove mushrooms from skillet and add to pine nuts.

In same skillet, cook steaks over medium heat for 7 to 9 minutes, or until meat is well done, turning steaks over once. Pour wine around steaks. Cook for 5 to 7 minutes, or until liquid is reduced by half. Return pine nut mixture to skillet. Serve over hot cooked wild rice, if desired.

Nutritional information not available.

Venison with Blue Cheese Sauce

Louis Bignami – Moscow, Idaho

¼ cup all-purpose flour
¼ teaspoon salt
⅛ teaspoon pepper
6 boneless venison loin steaks or substitute
    (4 oz. each), ½ inch thick
¼ cup margarine or butter, divided
2 tablespoons olive oil
½ cup dry red wine
¼ cup chopped shallots
2 tablespoons water
1 teaspoon snipped fresh
    marjoram or ½ teaspoon dried
    marjoram leaves
½ teaspoon instant beef
    bouillon granules
4 oz. crumbled blue cheese

6 servings

In shallow dish, combine flour, salt and pepper. Dredge steaks in flour mixture to coat. In 12-inch nonstick skillet, heat 2 tablespoons margarine and the oil over medium heat. Add steaks. Cook for 6 to 8 minutes, or until meat is desired doneness, turning steaks over once. Transfer steaks to warm platter. Cover to keep warm. Set aside.

To same skillet, add wine, shallots, water, marjoram and bouillon. Cook over medium-high heat for 1 to 2 minutes, or until mixture is reduced by half, stirring constantly. Add remaining 2 tablespoons margarine and the blue cheese. Cook over medium heat for 3 to 5 minutes, or until sauce is smooth, stirring constantly. Spoon sauce over steaks.

Per Serving: Calories: 299 • Protein: 28 g. • Carbohydrate: 6 g. • Fat: 16 g. • Cholesterol: 100 mg. • Sodium: 375 mg.
Exchanges: ¼ starch, 3¾ lean meat, ½ vegetable, 1 fat

Lemon-Garlic Venison Tenderloin

Keith Sutton – Benton, Arkansas

2 teaspoons snipped fresh parsley
1 clove garlic, minced
½ teaspoon grated lemon peel
½ teaspoon freshly cracked peppercorns
1 tablespoon olive oil
⅛ teaspoon salt
1 venison tenderloin or substitute (8 oz.), cut in half crosswise

2 servings

In small mixing bowl, combine parsley, garlic, peel and pepper. Rub steaks evenly on both sides with parsley mixture. Let stand at room temperature for 15 minutes.

In 10-inch nonstick skillet, heat oil over medium heat. Sprinkle salt over oil. Add steaks. Cook for 6 to 8 minutes, or until meat is desired doneness, turning steaks over once. Serve with baked potato and salad, if desired.

Per Serving: Calories: 200 • Protein: 26 g.
• Carbohydrate: 1 g. • Fat: 10 g.
• Cholesterol: 96 mg. • Sodium: 197 mg.
Exchanges: 3½ lean meat

Elk Tenderloin Forestière ↑

Louis Bignami – Moscow, Idaho

1½ -lb. elk tenderloin or substitute, cut into ½-inch-thick steaks
6 slices bacon
6 tablespoons margarine or butter, divided
8 oz. fresh mushrooms, sliced (3 cups)
2 tablespoons chopped shallots
2 cups beef broth
1 cup dry red wine
3 tablespoons all-purpose flour
1 teaspoon dried thyme leaves
¼ teaspoon salt
¼ teaspoon pepper

6 servings

Pound steaks to ¼-inch thickness with meat mallet. Set aside. In 12-inch nonstick skillet, cook bacon over medium heat until brown and crisp. Drain on paper-towel-lined plate. Cool slightly. Crumble bacon. Set aside. Wipe out skillet with paper towels. Set aside.

In 2-quart saucepan, melt 3 tablespoons margarine over medium heat. Add mushrooms and shallots. Cook for 3 to 5 minutes, or until tender, stirring frequently. Add broth and wine. Bring to a boil over high heat. Reduce heat to medium. Cook for 30 to 40 minutes, or until sauce is reduced to 2 cups, stirring frequently. Stir in bacon. Remove from heat. Set sauce aside.

On sheet of wax paper, combine flour, thyme, salt and pepper. Dredge steaks in flour mixture to coat. In same skillet, melt remaining 3 tablespoons margarine over medium heat. Add steaks. Cook for 4 to 6 minutes, or until meat is desired doneness, turning steaks over once. Transfer steaks to warm platter. Spoon sauce over steaks. Serve with hot buttered noodles, if desired.

Per Serving: Calories: 296 • Protein: 30 g. • Carbohydrate: 6 g. • Fat: 16 g.
• Cholesterol: 68 mg. • Sodium: 675 mg.
Exchanges: 3 lean meat, 1 vegetable, 1½ fat

Roulade of Moose

"This recipe was given to me by Shawn Rideout, camp cook at Conne River Outfitters in Newfoundland, Canada. It's delicious!"
Buck Taylor – Louisville, Alabama

STUFFING:

    5   slices bacon, chopped
    2   cups unseasoned dry bread crumbs
    ⅓   cup margarine or butter, melted
    ⅓   cup chopped onion
    ¾   teaspoon dried summer savory

1½ -lb. boneless moose round steak or substitute,
        cut into 6 serving-size pieces, pounded
        to ¼-inch thickness
    ¼   cup margarine or butter
    3   tablespoons all-purpose flour
    ¼   teaspoon salt
    ¼   teaspoon pepper
1¼   cups beef broth
    1   clove garlic, minced
    6   oz. fresh mushrooms, sliced (about 2 cups)
    ⅓   cup dry red wine

6 servings

Heat oven to 350°F. In 10-inch nonstick skillet, cook bacon over medium heat until brown and crisp. Drain, reserving 2 tablespoons drippings. In medium mixing bowl, combine bacon and remaining stuffing ingredients. Spoon about ⅓ cup stuffing down center of each steak. Starting with shorter side, roll up steaks jelly roll style. Secure roulades with wooden picks.

In same skillet, heat reserved drippings over medium heat. Add roulades. Cook for 4 to 6 minutes, or until browned on all sides. Arrange roulades in 12 x 8-inch baking dish. Set aside.

In same skillet, melt ¼ cup margarine over medium heat. Stir in flour, salt and pepper. Blend in broth and garlic. Reduce heat to medium-low. Cook for 3 to 5 minutes, or until mixture thickens and bubbles, stirring constantly. Stir in mushrooms and wine. Spoon gravy over roulades. Cover with foil. Bake for 50 minutes to 1 hour, or until meat is tender. Remove and discard wooden picks before serving. Serve with hot cooked pasta, if desired.

Per Serving: Calories: 517 • Protein: 33 g. • Carbohydrate: 32 g. • Fat: 27 g. • Cholesterol: 75 mg. • Sodium: 961 mg.
Exchanges: 2 starch, 3 lean meat, ½ vegetable, 3½ fat

Venison Stir-fry

Pamela G. Weum – Hillman, Minnesota

MARINADE:

¼ cup soy sauce
3 tablespoons cornstarch
3 cloves garlic, minced
2 teaspoons ground ginger
1 teaspoon white pepper
1 teaspoon five-spice powder
½ teaspoon sesame oil

1 to 1½-lb. boneless venison loin or substitute,
   cut into 2 × 1 × ¼-inch strips
2 tablespoons vegetable oil
1 medium red or green pepper, cut into thin strips
1 medium onion, thinly sliced
1½ cups thinly sliced celery
1 cup thinly sliced carrots
1 cup fresh broccoli flowerets
1 cup fresh snow pea pods
1 medium jalapeño pepper, thinly sliced
1 teaspoon sesame oil
1 tablespoon toasted sesame seed

4 to 6 servings

In large mixing bowl, combine marinade ingredients. Add venison strips. Stir to coat. Cover with plastic wrap. Refrigerate 8 hours or overnight, stirring occasionally.

In 12-inch nonstick skillet or wok, heat vegetable oil over medium-high heat. Add meat mixture. Cook for 8 to 10 minutes, or until meat is desired doneness, stirring frequently. Using slotted spoon, remove meat from skillet. Cover to keep warm. Set aside.

To same skillet, add remaining ingredients, except sesame seed. Cook for 3 to 5 minutes, or until vegetables are tender-crisp, stirring frequently. Return meat to skillet. Sprinkle with sesame seed. Serve with hot cooked rice, if desired.

Per Serving: Calories: 245 • Protein: 25 g. • Carbohydrate: 16 g. • Fat: 9 g. • Cholesterol: 80 mg. • Sodium: 775 mg.
Exchanges: 2¾ lean meat, 3 vegetable

Venison & Sauerkraut over Noodles

Joan N. Cone – Williamsburg, Virginia

2 tablespoons vegetable oil
1½ lbs. venison stew meat
    or substitute (well
    trimmed), cut into
    1-inch cubes
1 can (16 oz.) Bavarian-style
    sauerkraut
2 cups water
1 small onion, sliced
1 pkg. (1.75 oz.) beefy
    mushroom soup mix
2 tablespoons packed
    brown sugar
2 tablespoons red wine
    vinegar
1 teaspoon soy sauce
½ teaspoon ground ginger
    Hot buttered noodles

4 to 6 servings

Heat oven to 350°F. In 6-quart ovenproof Dutch oven or stockpot, heat oil over medium-high heat. Add venison cubes. Cook for 3 to 5 minutes, or just until meat is browned, stirring frequently. Add remaining ingredients, except noodles. Mix well. Cover.

Bake for 1 to 1½ hours, or until meat is tender, stirring occasionally. Serve mixture over noodles. Garnish with snipped fresh parsley, if desired.

Per Serving: Calories: 238 • Protein: 28 g. • Carbohydrate: 14 g. • Fat: 8 g. • Cholesterol: 96 mg. • Sodium: 1022 mg. Exchanges: ⅔ starch, 3 lean meat, ½ vegetable

Venison Burgundy à la Malachosky ↑

Dennis P. Malachosky – PA Furnace, Pennsylvania

MARINADE:
½ cup chopped onion
¼ cup Burgundy wine
2 tablespoons lemon juice
2 tablespoons vegetable oil
2 cloves garlic, minced
¼ teaspoon freshly ground pepper
¼ teaspoon salt

1 - lb. boneless venison round
    steak or substitute, cut into
    ¾-inch cubes

2 tablespoons margarine or butter
8 oz. fresh mushrooms, cut into
    quarters
1 large onion, cut into ½-inch
    cubes
3 tablespoons all-purpose flour
1 cup beef broth
¾ cup Burgundy wine
1 tablespoon catsup
1 teaspoon bouquet sauce

4 servings

In large mixing bowl, combine marinade ingredients. Add venison cubes. Stir to coat. Cover with plastic wrap. Refrigerate 8 hours or overnight, stirring occasionally.

Heat oven to 300°F. Drain and discard marinade from meat. In 12-inch non-stick skillet, melt margarine over medium-high heat. Add meat. Cook for 5 to 8 minutes, or until meat is no longer pink, stirring frequently. Transfer meat to 3-quart casserole. Set aside.

To same skillet, add mushrooms and onion. Cook over medium heat for 2 to 3 minutes, or until vegetables are tender. Add vegetable mixture to meat.

Place flour in same skillet. Blend in remaining ingredients. Cook over medium heat for 3 to 5 minutes, or until sauce thickens and bubbles, stirring constantly. Pour sauce over meat and vegetable mixture. Stir to coat. Cover. Bake for 1 to 1½ hours, or until meat is tender, removing cover during last 15 minutes. Serve mixture over hot buttered noodles and garnish with fresh parsley, if desired.

Per Serving: Calories: 370 • Protein: 30 g. • Carbohydrate: 18 g. • Fat: 16 g. • Cholesterol: 96 mg. • Sodium: 530 mg. Exchanges: ¼ starch, 3 lean meat, 3 vegetable, 2 fat

Curried Wild Pig

Jan Knotts – Jamestown, Colorado

2 lbs. boar round steak (well trimmed), cut into 1-inch pieces
½ teaspoon meat tenderizer
¼ cup cornstarch
3 to 4 tablespoons curry powder
1 teaspoon salt
½ teaspoon garlic powder
¼ to ½ teaspoon crushed red pepper flakes
1 can (14½ oz.) chicken broth
3 tablespoons vegetable oil
2 cups fresh broccoli flowerets
2 cups sliced carrots (½-inch slices)
2 cups sliced celery (1-inch lengths)

6 to 8 servings

In medium mixing bowl, combine boar pieces and tenderizer. Stir to coat. Cover with plastic wrap. Chill 1 hour. In small mixing bowl, combine cornstarch, curry powder, salt, garlic powder and pepper flakes. Blend in broth. Set aside.

In 12-inch nonstick skillet or wok, heat oil over medium-high heat. Add broccoli, carrots and celery. Cook for 5 to 7 minutes, or until vegetables are tender-crisp, stirring frequently. With slotted spoon, remove vegetables from skillet. Set aside.

In same skillet, cook meat over medium-high heat for 3 to 5 minutes, or until browned, stirring frequently. Return vegetables to skillet. Stir to combine. Add broth mixture to skillet. Cook for 2 to 3 minutes, or until sauce is thickened and translucent, stirring constantly. Serve over hot cooked rice, if desired.

Per Serving: Calories: 257 • Protein: 27 g.
• Carbohydrate: 15 g. • Fat: 10 g.
• Cholesterol: N/A • Sodium: N/A
Exchanges: ½ starch, 3¼ lean meat, 1½ vegetable

Venison Oriental

Vicki J. Snyder – Columbus, Ohio

1 - lb. boneless venison loin or substitute, cut into 1½ × ½-inch strips
¼ cup soy sauce
2 cloves garlic, minced
1 teaspoon grated fresh gingerroot or ½ teaspoon ground ginger
2 tablespoons vegetable oil
1 cup diagonally sliced celery
½ cup green pepper chunks (½-inch chunks)
½ cup red pepper chunks (½-inch chunks)
½ cup diagonally sliced green onions
¾ cup water
1 tablespoon cornstarch
2 medium tomatoes, each cut into 8 wedges

4 to 5 servings

In medium mixing bowl, combine venison strips, soy sauce, garlic and gingerroot. Stir to coat. Cover with plastic wrap. Refrigerate 4 to 6 hours, stirring occasionally.

In 12-inch nonstick skillet or wok, heat oil over medium-high heat. Add meat mixture. Cook for 6 to 8 minutes, or until meat is desired doneness, stirring frequently. With slotted spoon, remove meat from skillet. Set aside. To same skillet, add celery, pepper chunks and onions. Cook for 3 to 5 minutes, or until vegetables are tender-crisp, stirring frequently. Return meat to skillet.

In small mixing bowl, combine water and cornstarch. Stir into meat and vegetable mixture. Cook for 1 to 2 minutes, or until sauce is thickened and translucent, stirring constantly. Stir in tomato wedges. Cook for 3 to 4 minutes, or until tomatoes are hot, stirring occasionally. Serve over hot cooked rice, if desired.

Per Serving: Calories: 196 • Protein: 23 g. • Carbohydrate: 8 g. • Fat: 8 g.
• Cholesterol: 77 mg. • Sodium: 897 mg.
Exchanges: 2¾ lean meat, 1⅔ vegetable

Szechuan Venison Stir-fry

Keith Sutton – Benton, Arkansas

2 tablespoons soy sauce

4 teaspoons dark sesame oil, divided

1½ teaspoons sugar

1 teaspoon cornstarch

1-lb. boneless venison round steak or substitute,
cut into 2 × ¼-inch strips

1 tablespoon finely chopped fresh gingerroot

2 cloves garlic, minced

¼ teaspoon crushed red pepper flakes

1 pkg. (8 oz.) fresh whole baby carrots,
cut in half lengthwise

1 small red pepper, cut into 1-inch chunks

¼ lb. fresh snow pea pods

2 tablespoons unsalted peanuts (optional)

4 servings

In medium mixing bowl, combine soy sauce, 2 teaspoons oil, the sugar and cornstarch. Add venison strips. Stir to coat. Set aside.

In 10-inch nonstick skillet or wok, heat remaining 2 teaspoons oil over medium-high heat. Add gingerroot, garlic and red pepper flakes. Cook for 30 to 45 seconds, or until garlic begins to brown, stirring constantly. Add carrots and pepper chunks. Cook for 2 to 3 minutes, or just until vegetables begin to soften, stirring constantly. Add pea pods and peanuts. Cook for 30 seconds, stirring constantly. Transfer vegetable mixture to warm platter. Set aside.

To same skillet, add half of venison strips. Cook for 3 to 4 minutes, or until meat is no longer pink, stirring constantly. Remove from skillet. Repeat with remaining venison strips. Return vegetable mixture and meat to skillet. Cook for 3 to 4 minutes, or until mixture is hot and vegetables are tender-crisp. Serve over hot cooked rice, if desired.

Per Serving: Calories: 233 • Protein: 28 g. • Carbohydrate: 12 g.
• Fat: 7 g. • Cholesterol: 96 mg. • Sodium: 594 mg.
Exchanges: 3 lean meat, 2½ vegetable

Wayne's Special Venison Meatloaf

"The piccalilli (a combination of finely chopped green tomatoes, onion, cabbage and green peppers that has been canned) adds a slightly different flavor to the meatloaf. The flavor is subtle and not overpowering."
    Wayne Chamberlain – Pequot Lakes, Minnesota

⅓ cup catsup
2 tablespoons barbecue sauce
2 tablespoons French dressing

MEATLOAF:
2 lbs. lean ground venison or
        substitute, crumbled
1 cup canned piccalilli or pickled
        mixed garden vegetables,
        rinsed and drained
½ cup chopped onion
½ cup coarsely crushed seasoned
        croutons
2 eggs, beaten
½ teaspoon seasoned salt

8 servings

Heat oven to 350°F. In small mixing bowl, combine catsup, barbecue sauce and dressing. Set aside. In large mixing bowl, combine 3 tablespoons catsup mixture and the meatloaf ingredients. Spray 9 × 5-inch loaf dish with nonstick vegetable cooking spray.

Press meatloaf mixture into prepared dish. Spoon remaining catsup mixture evenly over meatloaf. Bake for 1 to 1½ hours, or until meat is firm and no longer pink. Let stand for 10 minutes before slicing.

Per Serving: Calories: 364 • Protein: 24 g. • Carbohydrate: 7 g. • Fat: 26 g.
• Cholesterol: 154 mg. • Sodium: 555 mg.
Exchanges: ¼ starch, 3 medium-fat meat, 1 vegetable, 2 fat

Venison Burgers Français

Thomas K. Squier – Aberdeen, North Carolina

1   lb. lean ground venison or
     substitute, crumbled
½   cup seasoned dry bread crumbs
1   egg, beaten
1   tablespoon Dijon mustard
½   teaspoon dried chervil leaves
½   teaspoon dried parsley flakes
½   teaspoon dried thyme leaves
¼   teaspoon dried basil leaves
¼   teaspoon dried mint leaves
¼   teaspoon dried oregano leaves
¼   teaspoon dried sage leaves

4 servings

In medium mixing bowl, combine all ingredients. Shape mixture into four ½-inch-thick patties. Arrange patties on rack in broiler pan, or prepare grill for barbecuing. Place pan under broiler with surface of meat 3 to 4 inches from heat. Broil or grill for 8 to 10 minutes, or until meat is desired doneness, turning patties over once. Serve burgers on toasted garlic bread slices, if desired.

Per Serving: Calories: 375 • Protein: 25 g.
• Carbohydrate: 11 g. • Fat: 25 g.
• Cholesterol: 154 mg. • Sodium: 573 mg.
Exchanges: ¾ starch, 3 medium-fat meat, 2 fat

Chili-Pepper Deer Burgers with Lime Mayonnaise ↑

Keith Sutton – Benton, Arizona

2   cups hickory chips

LIME MAYONNAISE:
⅓   cup mayonnaise or salad dressing
1   teaspoon Dijon mustard
1   teaspoon lime juice
½   teaspoon grated lime peel

BURGERS:
2   lbs. lean ground venison or substitute, crumbled
⅓   cup sliced green onions
3   tablespoons plain nonfat or low-fat yogurt
2   tablespoons finely chopped jalapeño pepper
½   teaspoon salt
½   teaspoon pepper

8   oz. hot pepper cheese, cut into 8 slices
8   kaiser rolls
     Lettuce
     Sliced tomato

8 servings

Place wood chips in large mixing bowl. Cover with water. Soak chips for 1 hour. In small mixing bowl, combine mayonnaise ingredients. Cover with plastic wrap. Chill. In medium mixing bowl, combine all burger ingredients. Shape mixture into eight ¾-inch-thick patties.

Prepare grill for barbecuing. Drain hickory chips and sprinkle over hot coals. Arrange patties on cooking grate. Grill, covered, for 15 to 18 minutes, or until meat is desired doneness, turning patties over once.

Top each burger with 1 slice cheese. Grill for 2 to 3 minutes, or until cheese is melted. Serve on kaiser rolls with lime mayonnaise, lettuce and tomato slices.

Per Serving: Calories: 645 • Protein: 35 g. • Carbohydrate: 32 g.
• Fat: 41 g. • Cholesterol: 137 mg. • Sodium: 760 mg.
Exchanges: 2 starch, 4 medium-fat meat, ½ vegetable, 4 fat

Ground Game with Pepper Cognac Sauce

Louis Bignami – Moscow, Idaho

BURGERS:

2 lbs. lean ground venison
   or substitute, crumbled
½ cup finely chopped onion
¼ cup snipped fresh parsley
4 cloves garlic, minced
1 teaspoon salt
½ teaspoon pepper

3 tablespoons margarine or butter,
   divided

1 tablespoon olive oil
3 tablespoons finely chopped
   shallots or green onions
¼ cup Cognac
1 cup game broth or chicken broth
1 tablespoon canned green
   peppercorns, packed in brine,
   drained and divided
1 cup whipping cream
1 tablespoon lemon juice

8 servings

In medium mixing bowl, combine burger ingredients. Shape mixture into eight ¾-inch-thick patties. Set aside. In 10-inch nonstick skillet, heat 2 tablespoons margarine and the oil over medium-high heat. Add patties. Cook for 6 to 8 minutes, or until meat is desired doneness, turning patties over once. Transfer burgers to warm platter. Cover to keep warm. Set aside.

In same skillet, cook shallots over medium-high heat for 1 to 2 minutes, or until lightly browned. Add Cognac. Stir to loosen browned bits in skillet. Add broth and half of peppercorns. Cook for 4 to 5 minutes, or until mixture is reduced by half, stirring frequently. Stir in cream and remaining 1 tablespoon margarine. Reduce heat to low. Simmer for 3 to 5 minutes, or until sauce thickens and bubbles, stirring constantly. Stir in juice. Remove sauce from heat. Spoon over burgers. Garnish with remaining peppercorns.

Per Serving: Calories: 484 • Protein: 23 g. • Carbohydrate: 3 g. • Fat: 40 g.
• Cholesterol: 154 mg. • Sodium: 531 mg.
Exchanges: 3 lean meat, ½ vegetable, 6¼ fat

← Spicy Venison Pita Sandwiches

George C. and Kay Halazon – Manhattan, Kansas

BURGERS:

1½ lbs. lean ground venison or
   substitute, crumbled
⅓ cup unseasoned dry bread
   crumbs
1 egg
3 tablespoons chopped onion
1 tablespoon frozen orange
   juice concentrate, defrosted
1 tablespoon frozen pineapple
   juice concentrate, defrosted
3 cloves garlic, minced
1½ teaspoons grated fresh
   gingerroot
½ teaspoon fennel seed
½ teaspoon curry powder
¼ teaspoon cayenne

8 pita loaves (6-inch)

TOPPINGS:
   Sliced tomato
   Sliced cucumber
   Leaf lettuce
   Sliced onion
   Plain nonfat or low-fat yogurt

8 servings

In large mixing bowl, combine burger ingredients. Shape mixture into eight ½-inch-thick patties. Arrange patties on rack in broiler pan, or prepare grill for barbecuing. Place pan under broiler with surface of meat 3 to 4 inches from heat. Broil or grill for 8 to 10 minutes, or until meat is desired doneness, turning patties over once.

Make slit in one end of each pita. Place 1 burger and desired toppings in each pita.

Per Serving: Calories: 426 • Protein: 23 g.
• Carbohydrate: 39 g. • Fat: 19 g.
• Cholesterol: 103 mg. • Sodium: 404 mg.
Exchanges: 2¼ starch, 2½ lean meat,
⅓ fruit, 2 fat

Moose Meatballs with Cranberry Barbecue Sauce

Edward Arsenault – Rumford, Maine

MEATBALLS:

- 2 lbs. lean ground moose or substitute, crumbled
- 1 cup cornflake crumbs
- 2 eggs
- ¼ cup snipped fresh parsley
- 2 tablespoons soy sauce
- ½ teaspoon garlic powder
- ½ teaspoon pepper

SAUCE:

- 1 can (16 oz.) whole-berry cranberry sauce
- 1 bottle (12 oz.) chili sauce
- ⅓ cup catsup
- 2 tablespoons packed brown sugar
- 1 tablespoon lemon juice
- 2 teaspoons instant minced onion

6 to 8 servings

Heat oven to 350°F. In large mixing bowl, combine meatball ingredients. Shape mixture into 42 meatballs, about 1½ inches in diameter. Arrange meatballs in single layer in 13 × 9-inch baking dish. Bake for 30 to 35 minutes, or until meatballs are firm and no longer pink, turning meatballs over once. Drain.

In medium mixing bowl, combine sauce ingredients. Pour over meatballs. Bake for 30 to 35 minutes, or until sauce is hot and bubbly and flavors are blended. Serve with hot cooked rice, if desired.

Per Serving: Calories: 526 • Protein: 25 g.
• Carbohydrate: 52 g. • Fat: 24 g.
• Cholesterol: 131 mg. • Sodium: 1213 mg.
Exchanges: ¾ starch, 2¾ lean meat,
1½ vegetable, 2¼ fruit, 3 fat

Norwegian Meatballs

Bill Stevens – Anoka, Minnesota

MEATBALLS:

1½ lbs. lean ground venison or substitute, crumbled
½ cup unseasoned dry bread crumbs
⅓ cup finely chopped onion
1 egg
1 teaspoon sugar
½ teaspoon salt
¼ teaspoon pepper
⅛ teaspoon ground allspice
⅛ teaspoon ground nutmeg

1 tablespoon margarine or butter
2 tablespoons all-purpose flour
½ teaspoon salt
¼ teaspoon ground nutmeg
⅛ teaspoon pepper
1 can (12 oz.) evaporated skim milk

6 servings

In large mixing bowl, combine meatball ingredients. Shape mixture into 48 meatballs, about 1 inch in diameter.

In 12-inch nonstick skillet, melt margarine over medium heat. Add meatballs. Cook for 10 to 15 minutes, or until meatballs are firm and no longer pink, stirring occasionally. With slotted spoon, remove meatballs from skillet. Cover to keep warm. Set aside.

Reduce heat to medium-low. To same skillet, add flour, ½ teaspoon salt, ¼ teaspoon nutmeg and ⅛ teaspoon pepper. Blend in milk. Cook for 8 to 10 minutes, or until sauce thickens and bubbles, stirring constantly. Return meatballs to sauce. Stir gently to coat. Serve with hot cooked noodles or rice, if desired.

Per Serving: Calories: 427 • Protein: 29 g.
• Carbohydrate: 17 g. • Fat: 26 g.
• Cholesterol: 139 mg. • Sodium: 596 mg.
Exchanges: 3 medium-fat meat,
2 vegetable, ½ milk, 2¼ fat

Sweet Italian Meatballs

Donna R. White and Kenneth R. White – Independence, Missouri

1 lb. lean ground venison or substitute, crumbled
½ lb. ground pork, crumbled
1 egg, beaten
¼ cup unseasoned dry bread crumbs
1 clove garlic, minced
1 teaspoon fennel seed
1 teaspoon grated lemon peel
1 teaspoon dried parsley flakes

¾ teaspoon pepper
½ teaspoon salt
⅛ teaspoon ground nutmeg
2 cartons (10 oz. each) prepared refrigerated Alfredo sauce
¼ cup shredded fresh Parmesan cheese
1 tablespoon snipped fresh parsley

4 to 6 servings

Heat oven to 350°F. In large mixing bowl, combine all ingredients, except Alfredo sauce, Parmesan cheese and parsley. Shape mixture into 32 meatballs, about 1½ inches in diameter. Arrange meatballs in single layer in 13 × 9-inch baking dish. Bake for 25 to 30 minutes, or until meatballs are firm and no longer pink, turning meatballs over once. Drain.

Pour Alfredo sauce over meatballs. Bake for 15 to 20 minutes, or until sauce is hot and bubbly. Sprinkle with Parmesan cheese and parsley. Serve over hot cooked linguine, if desired.

Per Serving: Calories: 679 • Protein: 30 g. • Carbohydrate: 9 g. • Fat: 59 g.
• Cholesterol: 224 mg. • Sodium: 1172 mg.
Exchanges: ½ starch, 4 lean meat, 9¼ fat

Barbecued Venison Meatballs

Gayle Grossman – Little Moran Hunting Club, Staples, Minnesota

MEATBALLS:

- 1 lb. lean ground venison or substitute, crumbled
- ½ cup crushed garlic-and-herb-seasoned croutons
- 1 egg
- ¼ cup milk
- 2 tablespoons chopped onion
- 1 tablespoon Worcestershire sauce
- 2 teaspoons catsup
- 1 teaspoon salt

SAUCE:

- 2 cups catsup
- ½ cup mild salsa
- ½ cup packed brown sugar
- ⅓ cup chopped onion
- 2 tablespoons Worcestershire sauce
- 2 tablespoons dark molasses
- ½ teaspoon dry mustard

4 to 6 servings

Heat oven to 400°F. In large mixing bowl, combine meatball ingredients. Shape mixture into 20 meatballs, about 1½ inches in diameter. Arrange meatballs in single layer in 13 × 9-inch baking dish. Bake for 15 to 20 minutes, or until meatballs are firm and no longer pink, turning meatballs over once. Drain.

In medium mixing bowl, combine sauce ingredients. Pour over meatballs. Bake for 10 to 15 minutes, or until sauce is hot and bubbly. Serve with hot cooked rice or mashed potatoes, if desired.

Per Serving: Calories: 446 • Protein: 18 g.
• Carbohydrate: 54 g. • Fat: 18 g.
• Cholesterol: 104 mg. • Sodium: 1708 mg.
Exchanges: ½ starch, 2 lean meat, 4 vegetable, 1½ fruit, 2½ fat

Cheddar-filled Venison Roll ↑

"This easy make-ahead hamburger is different and delicious."
John and Denise Phillips – Fairfield, Alabama

- 1½ lbs. lean ground venison or substitute, crumbled
- ½ cup unseasoned dry bread crumbs
- 1 egg
- ¼ cup barbecue sauce, divided
- ½ teaspoon salt
- ¼ teaspoon pepper
- 1 cup shredded Cheddar cheese
- ¼ cup sliced green onions

8 servings

Heat oven to 350°F. Lightly grease 12 × 8-inch baking dish. Set aside. In medium mixing bowl, combine ground venison, bread crumbs, egg, 2 tablespoons barbecue sauce, the salt and pepper. On sheet of wax paper, shape meat mixture into 14 × 8-inch rectangle.

Sprinkle cheese and onions evenly over meat mixture to within 1 inch of edges. Starting with short side, roll up tightly, peeling back wax paper while rolling. Discard wax paper. Pinch ends and seam of venison roll to seal.

Place venison roll seam-side-down in prepared baking dish. Bake for 1 to 1½ hours, or until meat is firm and no longer pink. Spoon remaining 2 tablespoons barbecue sauce evenly over meatloaf. Bake for 10 minutes. Let stand for 10 minutes before slicing. Serve slices in lettuce-lined hamburger buns, if desired.

Per Serving: Calories: 322 • Protein: 21 g. • Carbohydrate: 6 g. • Fat: 23 g.
• Cholesterol: 117 mg. • Sodium: 390 mg.
Exchanges: ⅓ starch, 3 medium-fat meat, 1½ fat

Mexican Torte →

John and Denise Phillips – Fairfield, Alabama

1 lb. lean ground venison or
   substitute, crumbled
1 cup chopped onions
1 pkg. (2.5 oz.) taco seasoning mix
1 pkg. (10 oz.) frozen chopped
   spinach, defrosted and
   well drained
1 cup cottage cheese, drained
1 pkg. (16 oz.) hot roll mix
1 egg beaten with 1 teaspoon
   water

6 to 8 servings

Heat oven to 350°F. Lightly grease bottom and sides of 8-inch spring-form pan. Set aside.

In 10-inch nonstick skillet, combine ground venison and onions. Cook over medium heat for 6 to 8 minutes, or until meat is no longer pink, stirring occasionally. Drain. Stir in seasoning mix. Cook for 2 minutes, stirring frequently. Remove from heat. Set aside. In small mixing bowl, combine spinach and cottage cheese. Set aside.

Prepare hot roll mix as directed on package. Divide dough in half. On lightly floured surface, roll half of dough into 12-inch circle. Fit circle into prepared pan, pressing dough over bottom and up sides of pan. Spoon meat mixture evenly into dough-lined pan. Top evenly with spinach mixture. On lightly floured surface, roll remaining dough into 9-inch circle. Place over spinach mixture, tucking edges of dough down around inside of pan. Cut several 1-inch slits in top to vent.

Brush top of torte with egg mixture. Bake for 45 to 50 minutes, or until deep golden brown. Let torte stand for 10 minutes before removing sides of pan. Serve in wedges.

Per Serving: Calories: 420 • Protein: 22 g.
• Carbohydrate: 48 g. • Fat: 14 g.
• Cholesterol: 81 mg. • Sodium: 1272 mg.
Exchanges: 3 starch, 1½ medium-fat meat, ½ vegetable, 1½ fat

Microwave Venison Goulash ↑

Joan N. Cone – Williamsburg, Virginia

1 lb. lean ground venison or
   substitute, crumbled
¾ cup chopped onion
1 can (15 oz.) stewed tomatoes,
   undrained
1 cup uncooked elbow macaroni
1 cup frozen corn
1 cup water
1 can (8 oz.) tomato sauce

1 teaspoon packed brown sugar
1 teaspoon chili powder
¼ teaspoon salt
¼ teaspoon pepper
¼ teaspoon ground cumin
1 tablespoon balsamic or red
   wine vinegar
½ cup shredded sharp Cheddar
   cheese

4 to 6 servings

In 3-quart microwave-safe casserole, combine ground venison and onion. Cover. Microwave at High for 4 to 6 minutes, or until meat is no longer pink, stirring twice to break apart. Drain. Add remaining ingredients, except vinegar and cheese. Mix well. Re-cover. Microwave at High for 17 to 19 minutes, or until macaroni is tender, stirring once or twice. Stir in vinegar. Sprinkle with cheese. Let stand, covered, for 3 to 5 minutes, or until cheese is melted.

Per Serving: Calories: 367 • Protein: 21 g. • Carbohydrate: 29 g. • Fat: 19 g.
• Cholesterol: 78 mg. • Sodium: 596 mg.
Exchanges: 1¼ starch, 2 lean meat, 2 vegetable, 2½ fat

Montana's Best Venison Pasties

Jerry L. Smalley – Columbia Falls, Montana

4½ cups all-purpose flour
1 teaspoon salt
1½ cups shortening
¾ cup cold water

FILLING:
½ lb. lean ground venison or
    substitute, crumbled
1½ cups cubed red potatoes
    (¼-inch cubes)
½ cup chopped carrot
1 small onion, thinly sliced
¼ cup thinly sliced celery
2 tablespoons snipped fresh
    parsley
½ teaspoon pepper
½ teaspoon salt
¼ teaspoon dried thyme leaves

2 tablespoons margarine or
    butter, melted

8 servings

In large mixing bowl, combine flour and 1 teaspoon salt. Cut in shortening until mixture resembles coarse crumbs. Sprinkle with water, 1 tablespoon at a time, mixing with fork until particles are moistened and cling together. Shape dough into ball. Wrap with plastic wrap. Chill 30 minutes.

Heat oven to 375°F. In 10-inch nonstick skillet, cook ground venison over medium heat for 3 to 5 minutes, or until meat is no longer pink, stirring frequently. Stir in remaining filling ingredients. Remove from heat. Set aside.

Divide dough into 16 equal portions. On lightly floured surface, roll each portion into 6-inch circle. (Keep dough covered with plastic wrap before and after rolling.) To assemble, place 2 tablespoons meat mixture slightly off center on 1 dough circle. Moisten edges of circle with water. Fold dough over filling to form half circle. Press edges together with tines of fork to seal. Place pasty on ungreased baking sheet.

Repeat with remaining dough circles and filling. Brush tops of pasties with margarine. Bake for 20 to 25 minutes, or until golden brown.

Per Serving: Calories: 728 • Protein: 13 g. • Carbohydrate: 61 g. • Fat: 48 g.
• Cholesterol: 25 mg. • Sodium: 467 mg.
Exchanges: 3½ starch, ¾ medium-fat meat, 1 vegetable, 8 fat

Venison Burritos

Shannon Hendrickson – Greenbush, Minnesota

- 2 lbs. lean ground venison or substitute, crumbled
- 1 can (16 oz.) refried beans
- 1 can (15 oz.) tomato sauce
- 1 cup chopped onions
- 1 cup shredded Cheddar cheese
- 1 can (4 oz.) chopped green chilies, drained
- 1½ teaspoons chili powder
- ½ teaspoon ground cumin
- ½ teaspoon pepper
- ¼ teaspoon ground cloves
- 16 flour tortillas (10-inch)

TOPPINGS:

Shredded lettuce
Shredded Cheddar cheese
Salsa
Sour cream

16 servings

Heat oven to 350°F. In 12-inch nonstick skillet, cook ground venison over medium heat for 10 to 12 minutes, or until meat is no longer pink, stirring frequently. Drain. Stir in remaining ingredients, except tortillas and toppings. Reduce heat to medium-low. Cook for 30 to 40 minutes, or until flavors are blended, stirring occasionally.

Warm tortillas as directed on package. Place about ½ cup meat mixture in center of each tortilla. Fold bottom half of tortilla over filling. Fold sides over folded half of tortilla. Fold top half of tortilla over filling. Place burritos seam-side-down on baking sheet. Bake for 8 to 10 minutes, or until hot. Serve with desired toppings.

TIP: Individually wrap and freeze burritos for future use, if desired.

Per Serving: Calories: 400 • Protein: 20 g. • Carbohydrate: 39 g. • Fat: 18 g. • Cholesterol: 58 mg. • Sodium: 658 mg. Exchanges: 2½ starch, 1½ lean meat, ¼ vegetable, 2½ fat

Venison-stuffed Peppers ↑

Deborah J. Barber – Ashaway, Rhode Island

- 6 large yellow, red or green peppers
- 10 cups water
- 3 cans (14½ oz. each) diced tomatoes, undrained
- ¼ cup packed brown sugar
- 1½ lbs. lean ground venison or substitute, crumbled

- 2 cups cooked brown rice pilaf or brown rice
- ⅔ cup seasoned dry bread crumbs
- 1 tablespoon Worcestershire sauce
- 1 teaspoon Mrs. Dash® all natural seasoning
- 1 teaspoon hot red pepper sauce

6 servings

Heat oven to 350°F. Cut ½-inch slice from top of each pepper, reserving tops. Remove and discard seeds and membrane. Cut and discard thin slice from bottom of each pepper to allow peppers to stand upright. (Do not cut hole in bottom of pepper.) In 6-quart Dutch oven or stockpot, bring water to a boil over medium-high heat. Add peppers. Cook for 3 to 5 minutes, or until peppers are tender-crisp. Remove peppers from water. Drain. Arrange peppers upright in 13 × 9-inch baking dish.

In medium mixing bowl, combine tomatoes and sugar. In large mixing bowl, combine 1 cup tomato mixture and remaining ingredients. Spoon about 1¼ cups meat mixture into each pepper. Top with reserved pepper tops. Pour remaining tomato mixture around peppers. Bake for 1 to 1½ hours, or until meat is firm and no longer pink.

Per Serving: Calories: 525 • Protein: 28 g. • Carbohydrate: 49 g. • Fat: 24 g. • Cholesterol: 101 mg. • Sodium: 797 mg. Exchanges: 2 starch, 3 medium-fat meat, 2 vegetable, ½ fruit, 2 fat

South of the Border Bake

Lorraine Oslin – Brook Park, Minnesota

1   pkg. (8 oz.) refrigerated crescent roll dough
1   lb. lean ground venison or substitute, crumbled
¼   cup chopped onion
1   can (16 oz.) refried beans
1   cup sour cream
1   egg
2   teaspoons chili powder
½   teaspoon ground cumin
⅛   teaspoon garlic powder
1   cup shredded Cheddar cheese

TOPPINGS:
    Shredded lettuce
    Chopped tomato
    Sliced black olives
    Sliced green onions
    Salsa

Heat oven to 375°F. Unroll crescent roll dough. Place in 12 × 8-inch baking dish. Press dough over bottom and 1 inch up sides of dish. Set aside. In 10-inch nonstick skillet, combine ground venison and onion. Cook over medium heat for 6 to 8 minutes, or until meat is no longer pink, stirring occasionally. Drain. Spoon meat mixture evenly over dough.

In medium mixing bowl, combine beans, sour cream, egg and seasonings. Spread bean mixture over meat mixture. Sprinkle evenly with cheese. Bake for 25 to 30 minutes, or until crust is golden brown. Top with desired toppings. Let stand for 5 minutes before cutting.

Per Serving: Calories: 441 • Protein: 22 g. • Carbohydrate: 24 g. • Fat: 29 g. • Cholesterol: 105 mg. • Sodium: 611 mg.
Exchanges: 1½ starch, 2¼ lean meat, ¼ vegetable, 4¼ fat

6 to 8 servings

Salisbury Venison Steaks

Ray Harper – Evansville, Indiana

1 can (10¾ oz.) condensed cream
   of mushroom soup
1 tablespoon prepared mustard
2 teaspoons Worcestershire sauce
1 teaspoon prepared horseradish
1½ lbs. lean ground venison or
   substitute, crumbled
½ cup unseasoned dry bread
   crumbs
½ cup chopped onion
1 egg, beaten
½ teaspoon salt
¼ teaspoon pepper
1 tablespoon vegetable oil
½ cup water
1 to 2 tablespoons snipped fresh
   parsley

6 servings

In medium mixing bowl, combine soup, mustard, Worcestershire sauce and horseradish. Set aside. In large mixing bowl, combine ground venison, bread crumbs, onion, egg, salt, pepper and ¼ cup soup mixture. Shape mixture into six ½-inch-thick patties.

In 12-inch nonstick skillet, heat oil over medium heat. Add patties. Cook for 5 to 7 minutes, or until meat is browned, turning patties over once. Add remaining soup mixture and the water. Cover. Cook for 15 to 18 minutes, or until meat is desired doneness, stirring sauce occasionally. Garnish with parsley. Serve with mixed vegetables and hot cooked noodles or rice, if desired.

Per Serving: Calories: 426 • Protein: 25 g.
• Carbohydrate: 12 g. • Fat: 30 g.
• Cholesterol: 137 mg. • Sodium: 782 mg.
Exchanges: ¾ starch, 3 medium-fat meat, ¼ vegetable, 3 fat

Backwoods Lasagna ↑

"This is excellent frozen and reheated." John and Denise Phillips – Fairfield, Alabama

2½ lbs. lean ground venison or
   substitute, crumbled
½ cup chopped onion
2 cloves garlic, minced
2 cans (14½ oz. each) diced
   tomatoes, drained
1 cup chopped green pepper
1 can (8 oz.) tomato sauce
1 can (6 oz.) tomato paste
1 tablespoon snipped fresh parsley
1 teaspoon salt
1 teaspoon dried oregano leaves
½ teaspoon dried basil leaves
½ teaspoon freshly ground pepper
1 cup ricotta cheese, drained
1 cup cottage cheese, drained
1½ cups shredded mozzarella cheese
1½ cups shredded Swiss cheese
12 lasagna noodles (8 oz.), cooked
½ cup shredded fresh Parmesan
   cheese

8 servings

Lightly grease 13 × 9-inch baking dish. Set aside. In 12-inch nonstick skillet, cook ground venison, onion and garlic over medium heat for 8 to 10 minutes, or until meat is no longer pink, stirring frequently. Drain. Add tomatoes, green pepper, tomato sauce and paste, parsley, salt, oregano, basil and pepper. Bring mixture to a boil. Reduce heat to low. Cover. Simmer for 30 minutes. Remove from heat.

Heat oven to 350°F. In small mixing bowl, combine ricotta and cottage cheeses. In medium mixing bowl, combine mozzarella and Swiss cheeses. Arrange 4 lasagna noodles in single layer in bottom of prepared baking dish. Top with one-third of meat mixture. Drop half of ricotta cheese mixture by spoonfuls over meat mixture. Sprinkle evenly with one-third of mozzarella cheese mixture. Repeat layer once. Top with remaining noodles and meat mixture. Sprinkle evenly with remaining mozzarella cheese mixture and the Parmesan cheese. Bake for 40 to 45 minutes, or until lasagna is hot and bubbly and golden brown. Let stand for 10 minutes before serving.

Per Serving: Calories: 703 • Protein: 52 g. • Carbohydrate: 37 g. • Fat: 38 g.
• Cholesterol: 178 mg. • Sodium: 1225 mg.
Exchanges: 1½ starch, 6¼ lean meat, 2 vegetable, ¼ milk, 3¾ fat

Small Game

← Calamine Rabbit Pie

"Calamine is a crossroad in southern Wisconsin where we loved to chase rabbits."
Thomas J. Carpenter – Maple Grove, Minnesota

2 dressed wild rabbits or substitute
    (1½ to 2 lbs. each), cut up
4 cups water
1 medium onion, cut into quarters
1 clove garlic, minced
½ teaspoon salt
½ teaspoon pepper
¼ teaspoon cayenne
4 cups peeled, cubed red potatoes
    (4 medium), ½-inch cubes

2 cups sliced carrots
½ cup sliced celery
½ teaspoon dried sage or
    rosemary leaves

CRUST:
5 cups buttermilk baking mix
1⅔ cups milk
1 tablespoon margarine
    or butter, melted

6 servings

In 6-quart Dutch oven or stockpot, combine rabbit pieces, water, onion, garlic, salt, pepper and cayenne. Bring to a boil over medium-high heat. Reduce heat to low. Simmer for 1 to 1½ hours, or until meat is tender. Remove from heat. Remove rabbit pieces from broth. Cool slightly. Remove meat from bones. Discard bones. Return meat to broth. Stir in potatoes, carrots, celery and sage. Cook over low heat for 30 to 35 minutes, or until broth is reduced by half and vegetables are tender, stirring occasionally. Remove from heat. Set filling aside.

Heat oven to 425°F. Spray 13 × 9-inch baking dish with nonstick vegetable cooking spray. Set aside. In medium mixing bowl, combine baking mix and milk. Stir with fork until soft dough forms. Divide dough in half. On lightly floured surface, roll half of dough into 14 × 10-inch rectangle. Fit rectangle into prepared dish, pressing dough over bottom and up sides of dish. Spoon filling evenly into dough-lined dish.

On lightly floured surface, roll remaining dough into 13 × 9-inch rectangle. Place over filling. Roll edges of bottom and top crusts together. Flute edges or press together with tines of fork to seal. Cut several 1-inch slits in top crust to vent. Bake for 20 to 25 minutes, or until crust is golden brown. Brush crust with margarine. Let pie stand for 5 minutes before serving. Garnish with snipped fresh chives, if desired.

Variation: On lightly floured surface, roll dough for top crust to ½-inch thickness. Using floured 2 to 3-inch cookie cutters, cut leaf or rabbit shapes. Arrange shapes on top of filling, spacing at least 1 inch apart. Continue as directed above.

Per Serving: Calories: 793 • Protein: 58 g. • Carbohydrate: 90 g. • Fat: 21 g.
• Cholesterol: 181 mg. • Sodium: 1722 mg.
Exchanges: 5½ starch, 5½ lean meat, 1 vegetable, ¼ milk, ½ fat

Rabbit with Paprika

Vicki J. Synder – Columbus, Ohio

1 egg
1 teaspoon milk
⅓ cup all-purpose flour
1 tablespoon plus 2 teaspoons
    paprika, divided
½ teaspoon salt
¼ teaspoon pepper
2 dressed wild rabbits or substitute
    (1½ to 2 lbs. each), cut up
1 tablespoon margarine or butter
1 medium onion, thinly sliced
1 cup sour cream

4 servings

Heat oven to 350°F. In shallow dish, lightly beat egg and milk. In large plastic food-storage bag, combine flour, 2 teaspoons paprika, the salt and pepper. Dip rabbit pieces first in egg mixture and then add, a few at a time, to bag. Shake to coat.

In 12-inch nonstick skillet, melt margarine over medium heat. Add rabbit pieces. Cook for 8 to 10 minutes, or until meat is browned, turning occasionally.

Transfer rabbit pieces to 2-quart casserole. Cover. Bake for 1 to 1½ hours, or until meat is tender. Transfer rabbit pieces to warm platter. Cover to keep warm. Set aside. Reserve ¼ cup drippings from casserole.

In 10-inch nonstick skillet, heat reserved drippings over medium heat. Add onion. Cook for 2 to 3 minutes, or until tender, stirring occasionally. Reduce heat to medium-low. Stir in sour cream and remaining 1 tablespoon paprika. Cook for 2 to 3 minutes, or until sauce is hot, stirring constantly. Spoon sauce over rabbit pieces. Garnish with sprigs of Italian parsley, if desired.

Per Serving: Calories: 593 • Protein: 75 g.
• Carbohydrate: 16 g. • Fat: 24 g.
• Cholesterol: 336 mg. • Sodium: 515 mg.
Exchanges: ½ starch, 9 lean meat,
1½ vegetable

Sour Cream Rabbit with Herbs

William W. Alexander – Duncan, Oklahoma

⅓ cup plus 1 tablespoon all-purpose
   flour, divided
½ teaspoon salt
½ teaspoon freshly ground pepper
2 dressed wild rabbits or substitute
   (1½ to 2 lbs. each), cut up
3 tablespoons margarine or butter
3 tablespoons olive oil
4 medium onions, cut into ½-inch
   slices
2 cups plus 2 tablespoons water,
   divided
1 tablespoon tomato paste
2 teaspoons instant beef bouillon
   granules
¼ cup sour cream
1 tablespoon snipped fresh parsley
2 teaspoons snipped fresh dill
   weed

4 servings

In large plastic food-storage bag, combine ⅓ cup flour, the salt and pepper. Add rabbit pieces, a few at a time, to bag. Shake to coat. In 12-inch nonstick skillet, heat margarine and oil over medium heat. Add rabbit pieces. Cook for 8 to 10 minutes, or until meat is browned, turning occasionally. Remove rabbit pieces from skillet. Set aside.

In same skillet, cook onion slices for 5 to 7 minutes, or until tender, stirring frequently. Add 2 cups water, the tomato paste and bouillon. Bring to a boil. Return rabbit pieces to skillet. Reduce heat to low. Cover. Simmer for 1 to 1½ hours, or until meat is tender. Transfer rabbit pieces to warm platter. Cover to keep warm. Set aside.

In small bowl, combine remaining 1 tablespoon flour and 2 tablespoons water. Stir flour mixture into liquid in skillet. Cook over medium heat for 3 to 5 minutes, or until mixture thickens and bubbles, stirring constantly. Remove from heat. Stir in sour cream, parsley and dill weed. Pour over rabbit pieces. Serve with hot cooked noodles or rice, if desired.

Variation: Sour Cream Squirrel: Follow recipe as directed, except substitute 3 to 5 squirrels for rabbits. Omit parsley and dill weed. Increase tomato paste to 2 tablespoons and add 1 teaspoon dried oregano leaves, 1 teaspoon chili powder and ⅛ teaspoon garlic powder.

Per Serving: Calories: 676 • Protein: 74 g. • Carbohydrate: 26 g. • Fat: 30 g.
• Cholesterol: 264 mg. • Sodium: 999 mg.
Exchanges: ¾ starch, 9 lean meat, 3 vegetable, ½ fat

Rabbit Provençale

*"This family recipe can be done ahead of
time to suit today's harried cooks."*
Louis Bignami – Moscow, Idaho

MARINADE:

1 cup Merlot or other dry red wine
1 cup sliced carrots
1 cup chopped onions
½ cup snipped fresh parsley
¼ cup olive oil
4 cloves garlic, minced
2 teaspoons dried thyme leaves
2 bay leaves

2 dressed wild rabbits or substitute
  (1½ to 2 lbs. each), cut up

SAUCE:

1 can (14½ oz.) diced tomatoes,
  undrained
3 to 4 tablespoons tomato paste
3 tablespoons Dijon mustard
1 teaspoon dried sage
1 teaspoon instant chicken
  bouillon granules

¼ cup olive oil

4 servings

In large plastic food-storage bag,
combine marinade ingredients.
Add rabbit pieces. Secure bag.
Turn to coat. Refrigerate 8 hours
or overnight, turning occasionally.

Heat oven to 350°F. Drain and
reserve marinade from rabbit
pieces. Set rabbit pieces aside. In
medium mixing bowl, combine
reserved marinade and the sauce
ingredients. Set aside.

In 6-quart Dutch oven or stockpot,
heat oil over medium heat. Add
rabbit pieces. Cook for 8 to 10
minutes, or until meat is browned,
turning occasionally. Pour sauce
mixture over rabbit pieces. Cover.
Bake for 1 to 1½ hours, or until
meat is tender. Serve over hot buttered egg noodles and garnish with
sprigs of fresh thyme or snipped
fresh parsley, if desired.

Per Serving: Calories: 691 • Protein: 72 g.
• Carbohydrate: 18 g. • Fat: 36 g.
• Cholesterol: 257 mg. • Sodium: 1035 mg.
Exchanges: 9 lean meat, 4 vegetable,
1¾ fat

Rabbit Hunter-style ↑

"Sourdough bread or white rice makes a fine accompaniment for this savory dish."
Ned Pendergast – San Francisco, California

2 tablespoons olive oil
2 dressed wild rabbits or substitute
  (1½ to 2 lbs. each), cut up
1 medium onion, cut into ½-inch
  chunks
1 cup sliced celery (½-inch slices)
½ cup sliced carrot (½-inch slices)

3 cloves garlic, minced
1 can (8 oz.) tomato sauce
¼ cup dry white wine
2 tablespoons quartered
  Spanish-style olives
1 tablespoon capers

4 servings

In 12-inch nonstick skillet, heat oil over medium heat. Add rabbit pieces.
Cook for 8 to 10 minutes, or until meat is browned, turning occasionally.
Remove rabbit pieces from skillet. Set aside.

In same skillet, cook onion, celery, carrot and garlic over medium-high heat
for 3 to 5 minutes, or until vegetables are tender-crisp, stirring frequently.

Add rabbit pieces and tomato sauce. Mix well. Reduce heat to low. Cover.
Simmer for 1 to 1½ hours, or until meat is tender. Add wine, olives and
capers. Simmer for 5 minutes to blend flavors.

Per Serving: Calories: 484 • Protein: 71 g. • Carbohydrate: 11 g. • Fat: 15 g.
• Cholesterol: 257 mg. • Sodium: 692 mg.
Exchanges: 8 lean meat, 2 vegetable

Rabbit Curry ↑

Jay "D" Flattum – Lofton Ridge Deer Farm, Chisago City, Minnesota

¾ cup all-purpose flour, divided
1 teaspoon salt, divided
¼ teaspoon pepper
2 dressed wild rabbits or substitute
   (1½ to 2 lbs. each), cut up
¼ cup margarine or butter
¼ cup vegetable oil
½ cup chopped onion
1 clove garlic, minced
1 medium red or green cooking
   apple, peeled, cored and chopped
½ cup thinly sliced carrot

½ cup chopped green pepper
2 teaspoons to 1 tablespoon curry
   powder
3 cups chicken broth
2 to 3 tablespoons lemon juice

CONDIMENTS:
   Sliced green onions
   Raisins
   Chopped peanuts
   Shredded coconut
   Chutney

4 servings

In large plastic food-storage bag, combine ½ cup flour, ½ teaspoon salt and the pepper. Add rabbit pieces, a few at a time, to bag. Shake to coat. In 12-inch nonstick skillet, heat margarine and oil over medium heat. Add rabbit pieces. Cook for 8 to 10 minutes, or until meat is browned, turning occasionally. Transfer rabbit pieces to warm platter. Cover to keep warm. Set aside.

Drain and discard all but 1 tablespoon drippings from skillet. Add onion and garlic. Cook over medium heat for 1 to 2 minutes, or until onion is tender, stirring constantly. Add apple, carrot, green pepper and curry powder. Cook for 2 to 3 minutes, or until vegetables are tender-crisp, stirring frequently. Stir in remaining ¼ cup flour and ½ teaspoon salt. Blend in broth. Add juice. Cook for 4 to 7 minutes, or until sauce thickens and bubbles, stirring constantly. Return rabbit pieces to skillet. Reduce heat to low. Cover. Simmer for 1 to 1½ hours, or until meat is tender. Serve rabbit pieces and sauce over hot cooked rice, if desired. Top with desired condiments.

Per Serving: Calories: 733 • Protein: 75 g. • Carbohydrate: 29 g. • Fat: 34 g.
• Cholesterol: 257 mg. • Sodium: 1592 mg.
Exchanges: 1¼ starch, 9 lean meat, ½ vegetable, ½ fruit, 1½ fat

Rabbit with Mustard Sauce

"I've also used this same technique with pheasant, and it's wonderful."
Teresa Marrone – Minneapolis, Minnesota

1 tablespoon margarine or butter
1 dressed wild rabbit or substitute
   (1½ to 2 lbs.), cut up
6 slices bacon, chopped
1 tablespoon Dijon mustard
1 tablespoon all-purpose flour
1 cup dry white wine
1 tablespoon white wine vinegar
½ teaspoon dried rosemary leaves,
   crushed
¼ teaspoon salt
¼ teaspoon pepper
½ cup sour cream

2 to 3 servings

Heat oven to 350°F. In 12-inch non-stick skillet, melt margarine over medium heat. Add rabbit pieces. Cook for 8 to 10 minutes, or until meat is browned, turning occasionally. Transfer rabbit pieces to 2-quart casserole. Set aside.

In same skillet, cook bacon over medium heat until brown and crisp. Drain on paper-towel-lined plate. Add bacon to casserole. Set aside. Drain and discard all but 1 tablespoon drippings from skillet. Stir in mustard and flour. Blend in wine and vinegar. Cook over medium-low heat for 3 to 5 minutes, or until sauce is slightly thickened, stirring constantly. Stir in rosemary, salt and pepper.

Pour sauce over rabbit pieces. Cover. Bake for 1 to 1½ hours, or until meat is tender. Transfer rabbit pieces to warm platter. Cover to keep warm. Set aside. Stir sour cream into sauce. Bake for 10 to 15 minutes, or until hot. Spoon sauce over rabbit pieces.

Per Serving: Calories: 481 • Protein: 52 g.
• Carbohydrate: 5 g. • Fat: 27 g.
• Cholesterol: 202 mg. • Sodium: 729 mg.
Exchanges: ½ starch, 7 lean meat, 1 fat

French-style Rabbit

Bob Hirsch – Cave Creek, Arizona

¼ cup olive oil
2 dressed wild rabbits or substitute
  (1½ to 2 lbs. each), cut up
1 can (15 oz.) tomato purée
4 oz. fresh mushrooms, thinly
  sliced (1½ cups)
1 cup chopped red pepper
⅓ cup oil-cured black olives,
  pitted and sliced
4 cloves garlic, minced
1 teaspoon dried thyme leaves
½ teaspoon salt
¼ teaspoon pepper
1 cup dry white wine

4 servings

In 6-quart Dutch oven or stockpot, heat oil over medium heat. Add rabbit pieces. Cook for 8 to 10 minutes, or until meat is browned, turning occasionally.

Add remaining ingredients, except wine. Cook for 30 minutes. Add wine. Bring to a boil. Reduce heat to low. Simmer for 30 to 45 minutes, or until meat is tender.

Per Serving: Calories: 585 • Protein: 72 g.
• Carbohydrate: 16 g. • Fat: 25 g.
• Cholesterol: 257 mg. • Sodium: 1252 mg.
Exchanges: 9 lean meat, 3 vegetable

Beer-braised Rabbit ↑

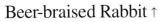

Jeff White – Fairfax Station, Virginia

2 dressed wild rabbits or
  substitute (1½ to 2 lbs. each),
  cut up
1½ teaspoons salt, divided
½ teaspoon freshly ground
  pepper, divided
3 tablespoons vegetable oil
3 medium red potatoes, cut into
  quarters
2½ cups diagonally sliced carrots
  (½-inch slices)
1 medium onion, sliced
1 can (12 oz.) beer, divided
¼ cup chili sauce
1 tablespoon packed brown sugar
1 clove garlic, minced
3 tablespoons all-purpose flour
⅓ cup water

4 to 6 servings

Sprinkle rabbit pieces evenly with ½ teaspoon salt and ¼ teaspoon pepper. In 6-quart Dutch oven or stockpot, heat oil over medium heat. Add rabbit pieces. Cook for 8 to 10 minutes, or until meat is browned, turning occasionally. Drain and discard oil from Dutch oven. To same Dutch oven, add potatoes, carrots and onion.

In small mixing bowl, combine 1 cup beer, the chili sauce, brown sugar and garlic. Pour over rabbit mixture. Bring to a boil over medium-high heat. Reduce heat to low. Cover. Simmer for 1 to 1½ hours, or until meat and vegetables are tender. Using slotted spoon, transfer rabbit pieces and vegetables to warm platter. Cover to keep warm. Set aside.

Add enough of remaining beer to broth in Dutch oven to equal 1½ cups (add water if necessary). In small bowl, combine flour and ⅓ cup water. Stir into broth. Cook over medium heat for 4 to 5 minutes, or until sauce thickens and bubbles, stirring frequently. Spoon sauce over rabbit pieces and vegetables.

Per Serving: Calories: 407 • Protein: 49 g. • Carbohydrate: 28 g. • Fat: 10 g.
• Cholesterol: 172 mg. • Sodium: 819 mg.
Exchanges: 1¼ starch, 5 lean meat, 1½ vegetable

Squirrel Pot Pie ↑

Frances Squier – Aberdeen, North Carolina

FILLING:
2½ cups cubed cooked squirrel or
    substitute (about 12 oz.)
2 cups peeled cubed red potatoes
    (2 medium), ½-inch cubes
1½ cups frozen peas and carrots
1 can (10¾ oz.) condensed
    cream of mushroom soup
½ cup thinly sliced celery
½ cup chopped onion
½ cup squirrel broth or chicken
    broth

½ teaspoon instant chicken
    bouillon granules
¼ teaspoon freshly ground pepper
CRUST:
¾ cup all-purpose flour
1 teaspoon baking powder
¼ teaspoon salt
¾ cup milk
½ cup margarine or butter, melted

6 servings

Heat oven to 375°F. Spray 8-inch square baking dish with nonstick vegetable cooking spray. Set aside. In 12-inch nonstick skillet, combine filling ingredients. Bring to a boil over medium-high heat. Remove from heat. Spoon filling evenly into prepared dish. Set aside.

In medium mixing bowl, combine flour, baking powder and salt. Add milk and margarine. Stir with fork just until dry ingredients are moistened. Spoon batter evenly over filling, spreading to edges. Bake for 30 to 35 minutes, or until crust is golden brown.

Per Serving: Calories: 411 • Protein: 20 g. • Carbohydrate: 32 g. • Fat: 23 g.
• Cholesterol: 59 mg. • Sodium: 1032 mg.
Exchanges: 2 starch, 2 lean meat, ½ vegetable, 3 fat

Jim's Saucy Crockpot Squirrel

James E. Collins – Alba, Pennsylvania

4 dressed squirrels or substitute
    (¾ to 1 lb. each), cut up
1 cup catsup
¾ cup water
½ cup packed brown sugar
⅓ cup Worcestershire sauce
1 teaspoon chili powder
3 to 4 drops red pepper sauce

4 servings

In 4-quart crockpot, combine all ingredients. Cover. Cook on High for 30 minutes. Reduce heat to Low. Cook for 6 to 8 hours longer, or until meat is tender. Serve over hot cooked rice, if desired.

Variation: Substitute 3 to 4 lbs. raccoon pieces for squirrel pieces.

Per Serving: Calories: 569 • Protein: 69 g.
• Carbohydrate: 47 g. • Fat: 11 g.
• Cholesterol: 264 mg. • Sodium: 1276 mg.
Exchanges: 9 lean meat, 3 vegetable, 2 fruit

One-pot Squirrel Dinner ↑

Joan N. Cone – Williamsburg, Virginia

- 1 pkg. (8 oz.) cream cheese, cut into 1-inch cubes, softened
- ¾ cup milk
- 1 pkg. (16 oz.) frozen broccoli, carrots and cauliflower, defrosted and drained
- 3 cups cooked rainbow fusilli or rotini
- 2 cups cubed cooked squirrel or substitute (8 to 10 oz.)
- 1 can (4 oz.) sliced mushrooms, drained
- 2 tablespoons Dijon mustard
- ½ teaspoon dried dill weed
- ¼ teaspoon salt
- ¼ teaspoon pepper
- ½ cup shredded fresh Parmesan cheese

6 to 8 servings

In 3-quart saucepan, combine cream cheese and milk. Cook over medium heat for 4 to 6 minutes, or until mixture is smooth, stirring constantly. Add remaining ingredients, except Parmesan cheese. Cook over medium-low heat for 5 to 7 minutes, or until mixture is hot, stirring occasionally. Sprinkle each serving evenly with Parmesan cheese.

Per Serving: Calories: 175 • Protein: 14 g. • Carbohydrate: 20 g. • Fat: 4 g. • Cholesterol: 35 mg. • Sodium: 382 mg.
Exchanges: 1 starch, 1⅓ lean meat, 1 vegetable

Squirrel Supreme

Mac Costello – Clinton, Indiana

- 2 tablespoons olive oil
- 2 dressed squirrels or substitute (¾ to 1 lb. each), cut up
- 1 large onion, thinly sliced
- 1 cup water
- 1 tablespoon dried sage leaves
- 2 cloves garlic, minced
- 1 teaspoon dried basil leaves
- 1 teaspoon dried parsley flakes
- 1 cup dry red wine

2 servings

In 10-inch nonstick skillet, heat oil over medium heat. Add squirrel pieces. Cook for 8 to 10 minutes, or until meat is browned, turning occasionally.

Add remaining ingredients, except wine. Reduce heat to low. Cover. Simmer for 1 to 1½ hours, or until meat is tender. Add wine. Cook, uncovered, over medium heat for 10 minutes. Serve over hot cooked rice, if desired.

Per Serving: Calories: 638 • Protein: 69 g. • Carbohydrate: 14 g. • Fat: 24 g. • Cholesterol: 264 mg. • Sodium: 338 mg.
Exchanges: 9 lean meat, 2 vegetable

Upland Game Birds

← Wild Turkey Breast & Pecans

"This is by far one of our favorite wild turkey recipes. The curry powder on the breast and the complementary vegetables and nuts mix with the brown and wild rice for a wonderful taste sensation."
Donna and Ken White – Independence, Missouri

¼ cup all-purpose flour
¾ teaspoon curry powder
¼ teaspoon seasoned salt
4 uncooked wild turkey breast slices (3 oz. each), ½ inch thick
2 tablespoons margarine or butter, divided

2 tablespoons olive oil, divided
¾ cup thinly sliced carrot
½ cup thinly sliced celery
1 cup pecan halves
¼ cup golden raisins (optional)
½ cup dry white wine

4 servings

In shallow dish, combine flour, curry powder and seasoned salt. Dredge breast slices in flour mixture to coat. In 12-inch nonstick skillet, heat 1 tablespoon margarine and 1 tablespoon oil over medium heat. Add breast slices. Cook for 3 to 5 minutes, or until meat is golden brown, turning over once. Transfer breast slices to warm platter. Set aside.

In same skillet, heat remaining 1 tablespoon margarine and 1 tablespoon oil over medium heat. Add carrot, celery, pecans and raisins. Cook for 5 to 8 minutes, or until vegetables are tender-crisp and pecans are toasted, stirring occasionally.

Arrange breast slices over vegetable mixture. Pour wine around breast slices. Cook for 5 to 8 minutes, or until vegetables are tender and liquid in pan thickens slightly. Serve with hot cooked brown and wild rice, if desired.

Per Serving: Calories: 446 • Protein: 24 g. • Carbohydrate: 14 g. • Fat: 31 g.
• Cholesterol: 53 mg. • Sodium: 207 mg.
Exchanges: ½ starch, 3 lean meat, 1 vegetable, 4½ fat

Roast Turkey with Corn & Sausage Stuffing

Keith Sutton – Benton, Arkansas

1 lb. unseasoned bulk pork sausage, crumbled
2 cups chopped onions
16 slices day-old bread, cut into ½-inch cubes (8 cups)
1 can (15 oz.) cream-style corn
1 tablespoon snipped fresh parsley
1½ teaspoons poultry seasoning
1 teaspoon salt
¼ teaspoon pepper
1 whole dressed wild turkey (10 to 12 lbs.), skin on

8 to 10 servings

Heat oven to 350°F. In 12-inch non-stick skillet, combine sausage and onions. Cook over medium heat for 6 to 8 minutes, or until meat is no longer pink and onions are tender, stirring occasionally. Drain, reserving ¼ cup drippings.

In large mixing bowl, combine sausage mixture, reserved drippings, the bread cubes, corn, parsley, poultry seasoning, salt and pepper.

Sprinkle cavity of turkey with additional salt and pepper. Spoon bread mixture lightly into cavity. Secure legs with string. Tuck wing tips behind back. Place turkey breast-side-up in roasting pan. Bake for 2½ to 3 hours, or until legs move freely and juices run clear.

Per Serving: Calories: 850 • Protein: 88 g.
• Carbohydrate: 31 g. • Fat: 39 g.
• Cholesterol: 256 mg. • Sodium: 1039 mg.
Exchanges: 1½ starch, 11½ lean meat, 1¾ vegetable, 1 fat

Mediterranean-style Quail with Sausage, Couscous & Red Pepper Sauce

Bruno G. Mella, Executive Chef – New York, New York

2 cups whipping cream
1 tablespoon vegetable oil
1 large clove garlic, minced
1 lb. bulk Italian sausage or
   chorizo, crumbled
6 whole dressed quail or substitute
   (4 to 6 oz. each), skin on
¼ teaspoon salt
¼ teaspoon freshly ground pepper
2 cups chicken broth
1 cup uncooked couscous
1 cup finely chopped green pepper
2 tablespoons unsalted butter
1 tablespoon snipped fresh thyme
   leaves
1 large red pepper
8 oz. steamed fresh green beans

4 servings

Per Serving: Calories: 1285 • Protein: 46 g.
• Carbohydrate: 48 g. • Fat: 101 g.
• Cholesterol: N/A • Sodium: 1562 mg.
Exchanges: 2¼ starch, 5 high-fat meat,
2½ vegetable, 12 fat

Heat oven to 425°F. Place cream in 2-quart heavy-bottomed saucepan. Cook over medium heat just until cream begins to simmer. Reduce heat to low. Simmer for 40 to 50 minutes, or until cream is reduced by half, stirring frequently with whisk. Set aside. Meanwhile, in 10-inch nonstick skillet, heat oil over medium heat. Add garlic. Cook for 1 to 2 minutes, or until golden brown. Add sausage. Cook for 6 to 8 minutes, or until meat is browned, stirring occasionally. Drain. Cool completely.

Sprinkle cavities of quail evenly with salt and pepper. Spoon sausage evenly into quail cavities. Arrange quail breast-side-up in shallow 12 × 8-inch baking dish. Bake for 25 to 30 minutes, or until meat is tender and juices run clear. Cover to keep warm. Set aside. Meanwhile, in 1-quart saucepan, bring broth to a boil over medium-high heat. Gradually stir in couscous. Add green pepper and butter. Boil for 2 minutes, or until broth is almost absorbed, stirring frequently. Remove from heat. Stir in thyme. Cover. Set aside.

Roast red pepper by spearing with meat fork and holding over gas flame of stovetop to blacken skin, or place on rack in broiler pan 4 to 5 inches from heat until skin blackens and blisters, turning frequently. Place roasted pepper in plastic food-storage bag. Secure bag. Let stand for 10 minutes. Remove and discard skin, stem and seeds. In food processor or blender, process reduced cream and red pepper until smooth. Cover to keep warm.

To serve, cut each quail in half. Place about ½ cup couscous in center of each serving plate. Pour red pepper sauce around couscous. Arrange 3 quail halves on top of couscous. Arrange hot green beans around quail. Garnish couscous with sprig of fresh thyme, if desired.

Quail That Won't Fail →

"Game hens also work well in this recipe, and Kansas doves were exquisite done this way. This sauce goes well with everything."
Bob Schranck – Golden Valley, Minnesota

4 whole dressed quail or substitute
   (4 to 6 oz. each), skin on
¼ teaspoon salt
¼ teaspoon pepper
2 tablespoons margarine or butter
2 tablespoons vegetable oil
¼ cup all-purpose flour
1 can (10½ oz.) condensed beef
   consommé
1 cup dry white wine
¼ teaspoon dried thyme leaves
2 bay leaves

4 servings

SPLIT each quail down the back and flatten.

Sprinkle salt and pepper evenly over quail. In 12-inch nonstick skillet, heat margarine and oil over medium-high heat. Add quail. Cook for 6 to 8 minutes, or until meat is browned, turning occasionally.

Remove quail from skillet. Reduce heat to medium. Stir flour into drippings in skillet. Blend in consommé, wine, thyme and bay leaves. Bring to a boil. Return quail to skillet. Reduce heat to low. Cover. Simmer for 30 to 40 minutes, or until meat is tender and juices run clear. Transfer quail to warm platter. Cover to keep warm. Set aside.

Cook sauce, uncovered, for 3 to 5 minutes longer, or until thickened, stirring constantly. Remove and discard bay leaves. Spoon sauce over quail. Serve quail with hot cooked white and wild rice, if desired.

Per Serving: Calories: 404 • Protein: 29 g.
• Carbohydrate: 8 g. • Fat: 28 g.
• Cholesterol: N/A • Sodium: 659 mg.
Exchanges: ½ starch, 4 medium-fat meat, 1½ fat

Greek Game Birds

Mike Moropoulos – Santa Barbara, California

1 cup all-purpose flour
1 tablespoon dried oregano leaves
2 teaspoons pepper
2 teaspoons paprika
½ teaspoon salt
8 whole dressed quail or substitute
   (4 to 6 oz. each), skin on
¼ cup olive oil
1½ cups lemon juice

8 servings

Heat oven to 400°F. In large plastic food-storage bag, combine flour, oregano, pepper, paprika and salt. Add quail, a few at a time. Shake to coat.

In 12-inch nonstick skillet, heat oil over medium heat. Add quail. Cook for 8 to 10 minutes, or until meat is browned, turning occasionally. Arrange quail breast-side-up in 13 × 9-inch baking dish. Pour lemon juice over quail. Bake for 30 to 40 minutes, or until meat is tender and juices run clear, basting frequently. Serve quail with rice or orzo pilaf, if desired.

Per Serving: Calories: 373 • Protein: 27 g. • Carbohydrate: 16 g. • Fat: 22 g.
• Cholesterol: N/A • Sodium: 214 mg.
Exchanges: 1 starch, 3¼ lean meat, ¼ fruit, 2½ fat

Roast Partridge with Figs & Garlic Sauce

William D. Gregoire – Minneapolis, Minnesota

2 whole dressed partridge or substitute (¾ to 1 lb. each), skin on
¼ teaspoon salt
¼ teaspoon pepper
1 tablespoon unsalted butter, softened
8 cloves garlic, unpeeled
8 oz. dried figs, stems removed, quartered
1 cup dry red wine
¼ cup finely chopped onion
1 tablespoon honey

GARLIC SAUCE:
¼ cup chicken broth
1 tablespoon bourbon
1 tablespoon whipping cream
3 tablespoons unsalted butter
¼ teaspoon salt
¼ teaspoon freshly ground pepper

4 servings

Heat oven to 350°F. Sprinkle partridge evenly with ¼ teaspoon salt and ¼ teaspoon pepper. Rub partridge with softened butter. Place in 10-inch ovenproof skillet. Add garlic. Bake for 40 to 50 minutes, or until meat is tender and juices run clear.

Meanwhile, in 2-quart saucepan, combine figs, wine, onion and honey. Cook over medium-low heat for 25 to 30 minutes, or until figs are tender and liquid is almost absorbed, stirring occasionally. Cover to keep warm. Set aside.

Remove partridge and garlic from skillet. Set aside. Drain and discard any drippings from skillet. In same skillet, combine broth, bourbon and cream. Remove skins from 4 cloves garlic. Mash garlic and add to cream mixture. Bring to a boil over medium heat. Add remaining sauce ingredients. Cook for 2 to 4 minutes, or until butter is melted and sauce is slightly thickened, stirring constantly.

Carve meat from partridge. Arrange slices on plate with figs and remaining 4 cloves garlic. Spoon garlic sauce over partridge.

Per Serving: Calories: 588 • Protein: 42 g. • Carbohydrate: 46 g. • Fat: 27 g.
• Cholesterol: 28 mg. • Sodium: 414 mg.
Exchanges: 5¾ lean meat, ½ vegetable, 2¾ fruit, 1¾ fat

Lemon Parmesan Doves

Thomas K. Squier – Aberdeen, North Carolina

6 whole dressed doves or substitute (2 to 3 oz. each), skin removed
¼ cup Italian seasoned dry bread crumbs
¼ cup shredded fresh Parmesan cheese
¼ cup snipped fresh parsley
1 teaspoon grated lemon peel
¼ cup margarine or butter, melted
¼ cup lemon juice

4 servings

Heat oven to 350°F. Split each dove down the back and flatten (see page 65). Set aside. In small mixing bowl, combine crumbs, Parmesan cheese, parsley and peel. In second small mixing bowl, combine margarine and juice.

Dip doves first in margarine mixture, then dredge in crumb mixture, pressing lightly to coat. Arrange doves breast-side-up in 12 × 8-inch baking dish. Drizzle remaining margarine mixture evenly over doves. Bake for 50 minutes to 1 hour, or until meat is tender and juices run clear.

Nutritional information not available.

Quail in Pear Nests ↑

"A decorative dish that's easy to fix, but impressive indeed."
Louis Bignami – Moscow, Idaho

4 large firm pears (10 oz. each)
   Ground cinnamon
   Ground nutmeg
8 whole dressed quail or substitute (4 to 6 oz. each), skin on
   Salt
   Pepper
¾ cup golden raisins
¾ cup brandy
3 tablespoons prepared honey mustard
½ cup dry white wine
⅔ cup whipping cream

8 servings

Cut each pear in half lengthwise. Remove cores. Partially scoop out insides of each pear half to make nest for each quail. Sprinkle inside of each pear half lightly with cinnamon and nutmeg. Set aside.

Pat quail dry inside and out with paper towels. Sprinkle cavity and outside of each quail lightly with salt and pepper. Place 1 quail breast-side-up in each pear half. Place in large mixing bowl. Add raisins. Drizzle brandy over quail and raisins. Cover with plastic wrap. Let stand at room temperature for 1 hour.

Heat oven to 425°F. Drain and reserve brandy from pear nests. Spoon raisins evenly into cavities of quail. Secure legs with string. Arrange pear nests in 10-inch ovenproof skillet. Spread thin layer of honey mustard evenly over each quail. Bake for 25 to 30 minutes, or until meat is tender and juices run clear. Transfer pear nests to warm platter. Cover to keep warm. Set aside.

To drippings in skillet, add reserved brandy and the wine. Place over medium-high heat. Stir in cream. Cook for 4 to 5 minutes, or until mixture is reduced by half, stirring constantly. Serve pear nests with hot cooked rice or pasta, if desired. Serve quail with sauce.

Per Serving: Calories: 505 • Protein: 26 g. • Carbohydrate: 33 g. • Fat: 23 g.
• Cholesterol: N/A • Sodium: 77 mg.
Exchanges: 3½ lean meat, 2¼ fruit, 4 fat

Dove à l'Orange

"Birds cooked like this will literally fall off the bone, and are moist and delicious!"
Buck Taylor – Louisville, Alabama

½ cup finely chopped red cooking
   apple
¼ cup finely chopped onion
8 whole dressed doves or substitute
   (2 to 3 oz. each), skin removed
2 tablespoons margarine or butter

ORANGE SAUCE:
¼ cup margarine or butter
¼ cup all-purpose flour
1 tablespoon sugar
½ teaspoon instant chicken
   bouillon granules
⅛ teaspoon garlic powder
⅛ teaspoon freshly ground pepper
⅛ teaspoon onion powder
1 cup water
¾ cup orange juice
¼ cup brandy

3 to 4 servings

Heat oven to 300°F. In small mixing bowl, combine apple and onion. Spoon apple mixture evenly into cavities of doves.

In 12-inch nonstick skillet, melt 2 tablespoons margarine over medium heat. Add doves. Cook for 3 to 5 minutes, or just until meat is lightly browned, turning occasionally. Arrange doves breast-side-up in 12 × 8-inch baking dish. Set aside.

In same skillet, melt ¼ cup margarine over medium heat. Stir in flour, sugar, bouillon, garlic powder, pepper and onion powder. Blend in water, juice and brandy. Cook for 5 to 6 minutes, or until sauce is slightly thickened, stirring constantly.

Pour sauce over doves in baking dish. Cover with foil. Bake for 1½ to 2 hours, or until meat is tender.

Nutritional information not available.

Southwestern Quail →

Thomas K. Squier – Aberdeen, North Carolina

1 can (14½ oz.) diced tomatoes, undrained
¾ cup sliced green onions
½ cup chopped green pepper
¼ cup mild salsa
1 clove garlic, minced
¼ teaspoon salt
¼ teaspoon pepper
4 whole dressed quail or substitute (4 to 6 oz. each), split in half, skin on
3 tablespoons all-purpose flour
2 tablespoons olive oil
1 ripe avocado, peeled and cut into 8 wedges
 Snipped fresh cilantro leaves

4 servings

In medium mixing bowl, combine tomatoes, onions, green pepper, salsa, garlic, salt and pepper. Set aside.

In large plastic food-storage bag, combine quail halves and flour. Shake to coat. In 10-inch nonstick skillet, heat oil over medium heat. Add quail halves. Cook for 5 to 7 minutes, or until meat is golden brown, turning over once.

Spoon tomato mixture over quail halves. Reduce heat to low. Cover. Simmer for 25 to 30 minutes, or until meat is tender and juices run clear.

Garnish quail halves with avocado wedges and cilantro. Serve quail with hot cooked rice, if desired.

Per Serving: Calories: 439 • Protein: 28 g.
• Carbohydrate: 16 g. • Fat: 30 g.
• Cholesterol: N/A • Sodium: 468 mg.
Exchanges: ¼ starch, 3 medium-fat meat, 2½ vegetable

Grouse & Wild Rice

"This recipe may be doubled, tripled, etc., but add only 2 cups water for each additional package of rice."

Edward C. Hanks – Tehachapi, California

2⅓ cups water
1 can (10¾ oz.) condensed cream of mushroom soup
¾ cup dry sherry
1 pkg. (5 oz.) long-grain white and wild rice mix
1 can (4 oz.) sliced mushrooms, undrained

1 tablespoon margarine or butter, melted
2 whole dressed ruffed grouse or substitute (1 to 1¼ lbs. each), split in half, skin removed

4 servings

Heat oven to 325°F. In 13 × 9-inch baking dish, combine all ingredients, except grouse halves. Arrange grouse halves wing-side-up over rice mixture. Cover with foil. Bake for 1 to 1½ hours, or until meat is tender and juices run clear, stirring rice mixture occasionally.

Remove foil. Bake for 30 to 40 minutes longer, or until rice is tender and liquid is absorbed. Serve grouse with tossed green salad or green vegetable, if desired.

Per Serving: Calories: 356 • Protein: 50 g. • Carbohydrate: 37 g. • Fat: 28 g.
• Cholesterol: N/A • Sodium: 1847 mg.
Exchanges: 2½ starch, 6 lean meat, 2 fat

Fried Quail

Ferne Holmes – Phoenix, Arizona

¾ cup all-purpose flour
1½ teaspoons seasoned salt
½ teaspoon pepper
8 whole dressed quail or substitute (4 to 6 oz. each), split in half, skin on
¼ cup margarine or butter
2 tablespoons finely chopped onion
⅔ cup water
1 can (5 oz.) evaporated milk
1 teaspoon instant chicken bouillon granules

8 servings

In large plastic food-storage bag, combine flour, seasoned salt and pepper. Add quail halves, a few at a time. Shake to coat. In 12-inch nonstick skillet, melt margarine over medium heat. Add quail halves. Cook for 25 to 30 minutes, or until meat is tender and juices run clear, turning occasionally. Transfer quail halves to warm platter. Cover to keep warm. Set aside.

To drippings in skillet, add onion. Cook for 30 seconds to 1 minute, or until tender, stirring frequently. Add water. Stir to loosen browned bits in skillet. Add milk and bouillon. Cook for 1 to 2 minutes, or until mixture begins to bubble, stirring constantly. Return quail halves to skillet. Stir to coat. Serve quail with hot cooked rice and garnish with snipped fresh parsley, if desired.

Per Serving: Calories: 364 • Protein: 27 g.
• Carbohydrate: 11 g. • Fat: 23 g.
• Cholesterol: N/A • Sodium: 509 mg.
Exchanges: ½ starch, 3½ lean meat, ¼ milk, 2½ fat

Grilled Birds with Chili-Peanut Sauce ↑

"Grilled birds – chukars, quail, pheasants or grouse — go nicely with this treatment."
Louis Bignami – Moscow, Idaho

MARINADE:
½ cup sliced green onions
½ cup soy sauce
1 teaspoon dry mustard
½ teaspoon dried rosemary leaves

4 whole dressed chukars or substitute (¾ to 1 lb. each), split in half, skin on

SAUCE:
¾ cup whipping cream
¼ cup creamy peanut butter
1 tablespoon dry sherry
¼ teaspoon crushed red pepper flakes

8 servings

In large plastic food-storage bag, combine marinade ingredients. Add chukar halves. Secure bag. Turn to coat. Refrigerate 5 hours or overnight, turning bag occasionally.

Drain and reserve marinade from chukar halves. Prepare grill for barbecuing. Spray cooking grate with nonstick vegetable cooking spray. Arrange chukar halves on prepared grate. Grill for 10 to 15 minutes, or until meat is tender and juices run clear, turning chukar halves over once and basting with reserved marinade every 5 minutes. Remove chukar halves from grill. Cover to keep warm. Set aside.

In 1-quart saucepan, combine sauce ingredients. Cook over medium heat for 5 to 7 minutes, or until sauce thickens and bubbles, stirring constantly. Spoon sauce onto serving plates. Arrange chukar halves on top of sauce. Garnish with additional sliced green onions or chopped peanuts, if desired.

Per Serving: Calories: 494 • Protein: 48 g. • Carbohydrate: 4 g. • Fat: 31 g.
• Cholesterol: N/A • Sodium: 1154 mg.
Exchanges: 6½ lean meat, ¾ vegetable, 2¼ fat

Grilled Pheasant Midwest →

Ray Harper – Evansville, Indiana

MARINADE:

- 1 cup apple juice
- ½ cup vegetable oil
- ¼ cup soy sauce
- ¼ cup packed brown sugar
- 3 tablespoons lemon juice
- 2 tablespoons shredded carrot
- 2 tablespoons snipped fresh parsley
- 2 cloves garlic, minced
- ½ teaspoon Worcestershire sauce
- 1 bay leaf
- 2 whole peppercorns

- 3 bone-in whole pheasant breasts or substitute (8 to 10 oz. each), split in half, skin removed
- 2 tablespoons olive oil
- 2 large carrots, cut into 2 × ¼-inch strips
- 2 medium zucchini, cut into 2 × ¼-inch strips
- 2 medium yellow summer squash, cut into 2 × ¼-inch strips

6 servings

In 13 x 9-inch baking dish, combine marinade ingredients. Place breast halves in baking dish in single layer. Turn to coat. Cover with plastic wrap. Chill 6 to 8 hours, turning breast halves over once. Drain and reserve marinade. Remove and discard bay leaf. Chill marinade.

Prepare grill for barbecuing. Spray cooking grate with nonstick vegetable cooking spray. Arrange breast halves on prepared grate. Grill for 15 to 20 minutes, or until meat is tender and juices run clear, turning breast halves over once and basting with reserved marinade every 5 minutes.

In 10-inch nonstick skillet, heat oil over medium heat. Add vegetable strips. Cook for 5 to 8 minutes, or until vegetables are tender-crisp, stirring occasionally. Serve pheasant with vegetables.

Per Serving: Calories: 376 • Protein: 26 g.
• Carbohydrate: 19 g. • Fat: 22 g.
• Cholesterol: N/A • Sodium: 578 mg.
Exchanges: 3⅓ lean meat, 1½ vegetable, ¾ fruit, 2¼ fat

Creamed Pheasant

"Fix any other game bird the same way. I do pheasant this way for 200 people!"
Linda Hehr – Kulm, North Dakota

- ⅓ cup all-purpose flour
- ½ teaspoon salt
- ½ teaspoon pepper
- ¼ teaspoon lemon pepper
- ¼ teaspoon garlic powder
- ¼ teaspoon paprika

- 1 dressed pheasant or substitute (1½ to 2¼ lbs.), cut up, skin removed
- 3 tablespoons vegetable oil
- 1 cup whipping cream

3 to 4 servings

Heat oven to 300°F. In large plastic food-storage bag, combine flour, salt, peppers, garlic powder and paprika. Add pheasant pieces. Shake to coat. In 10-inch nonstick skillet, heat oil over medium-high heat. Add pheasant pieces. Cook for 10 to 12 minutes, or until meat is browned, turning occasionally. Place pheasant pieces in 2-quart casserole. Pour cream over pheasant pieces. Cover. Bake for 1 to 1½ hours, or until meat is tender.

Per Serving: Calories: 668 • Protein: 44 g. • Carbohydrate: 10 g. • Fat: 49 g.
• Cholesterol: N/A • Sodium: 422 mg.
Exchanges: ⅔ starch, 5½ medium-fat meat, 4½ fat

Pheasant Italiano

Bob Schranck – Golden Valley, Minnesota

¼ cup all-purpose flour
¼ teaspoon salt
¼ teaspoon pepper
2 dressed pheasants or substitute (1½ to 2¼ lbs. each), cut up, skin removed
¼ cup olive oil
1¾ cups finely chopped green peppers
1¾ cups finely chopped onions
4 oz. fresh mushrooms, finely chopped (1 cup)
1 clove garlic, minced
2 cans (14½ oz. each) whole tomatoes, undrained and cut up
½ cup dry red wine
¼ cup snipped fresh parsley
1 teaspoon sugar
1 teaspoon dried oregano leaves
½ teaspoon dried rosemary leaves

6 to 8 servings

In shallow dish, combine flour, salt and pepper. Dredge pheasant pieces in flour mixture to coat. In 12-inch nonstick skillet, heat oil over medium-high heat. Add half of pheasant pieces. Cook for 10 to 12 minutes, or until meat is browned, turning occasionally. Transfer pheasant pieces to warm platter. Repeat with remaining pheasant pieces. Cover to keep warm. Set aside.

In same skillet, combine green peppers, onions, mushrooms and garlic. Cook over medium heat for 3 to 5 minutes, or until vegetables are tender, stirring occasionally. Stir in remaining ingredients, except pheasant pieces.

Arrange pheasant pieces, except breasts, over vegetables in skillet. Bring to a boil. Reduce heat to low. Simmer for 30 minutes, rearranging pheasant pieces once. Add pheasant breasts. Simmer for 15 to 30 minutes, or until meat is tender and juices run clear, rearranging pheasant pieces occasionally.

Per Serving: Calories: 449 • Protein: 44 g. • Carbohydrate: 12 g. • Fat: 24 g. • Cholesterol: N/A • Sodium: 312 mg. Exchanges: ¼ starch, 5 medium-fat meat, 1¾ vegetable

Johnny Appleseed Pheasant ↑

Julie Mertz – Dakota Hunting Farms, Hecla, South Dakota

½ teaspoon salt
¼ teaspoon freshly ground pepper
1 dressed pheasant or substitute (1½ to 2¼ lbs.), cut up, skin on
3 tablespoons margarine or butter
1 cup apple cider or apple juice
1 teaspoon ground cinnamon
2 small red cooking apples, cored and cut into ½-inch wedges

3 to 4 servings

Sprinkle salt and pepper evenly over pheasant pieces. In 10-inch nonstick skillet, melt margarine over medium-high heat. Add pheasant pieces. Cook for 10 to 12 minutes, or until meat is browned, turning occasionally. Drain and discard fat from skillet. In small mixing bowl, combine apple cider and cinnamon. Pour mixture over pheasant pieces. Bring to a boil. Reduce heat to low. Cover. Simmer for 30 minutes. Add apple slices. Re-cover. Simmer for 20 to 30 minutes, or until meat is tender and juices run clear.

Per Serving: Calories: 471 • Protein: 42 g. • Carbohydrate: 16 g. • Fat: 26 g. • Cholesterol: N/A • Sodium: 449 mg. Exchanges: 6 lean meat, 1 fruit, 1½ fat

72

Sun-kissed Pheasant →

"Years back, our family hunted with a chef from San Francisco. He whipped this up."
Annette Bignami – Moscow, Idaho

1 dressed pheasant or substitute
    (1½ to 2¼ lbs.), cut up, skin
    removed
⅔ cup all-purpose flour
3 tablespoons margarine or butter
3 tablespoons olive oil
    Juice from 3 large oranges or
    1½ cups prepared orange juice
1 cup dry white wine
½ cup golden raisins
1 tablespoon snipped fresh
    oregano leaves
1 tablespoon snipped fresh parsley
1 tablespoon snipped fresh
    rosemary leaves

3 to 4 servings

In large plastic food-storage bag, combine pheasant pieces and flour. Shake to coat. In 12-inch nonstick skillet, heat margarine and oil over medium-high heat. Add pheasant pieces. Cook for 10 to 12 minutes, or until meat is browned, turning occasionally. Transfer pheasant pieces to warm platter. Drain and discard fat from skillet.

In same skillet, combine remaining ingredients. Bring to a boil. Reduce heat to low. Return pheasant pieces to skillet. Cover. Simmer for 40 to 50 minutes, or until meat is tender and juices run clear. Serve over hot cooked rice, if desired.

Per Serving: Calories: 620 • Protein: 45 g.
• Carbohydrate: 41 g. • Fat: 30 g.
• Cholesterol: N/A • Sodium: 147 mg.
Exchanges: 1 starch, 6 lean meat, 1¾ fruit, 2½ fat

Gayle's Barbecued Pheasant

Gayle Grossman – Little Moran Hunting Club, Staples, Minnesota

1 cup all-purpose flour
1 teaspoon salt
½ teaspoon freshly ground pepper
¼ teaspoon garlic powder
2 dressed pheasants or substitute
    (1½ to 2¼ lbs. each), cut up,
    skin on
3 tablespoons vegetable oil
2 tablespoons margarine or butter

SAUCE:
1¾ cups catsup
½ cup salsa
½ cup finely chopped onion
⅓ cup packed brown sugar
2 tablespoons Worcestershire
    sauce
2 tablespoons dark molasses
½ teaspoon dry mustard

6 to 8 servings

Heat oven to 325°F. In shallow dish, combine flour, salt, pepper and garlic powder. Dredge pheasant pieces in flour mixture to coat. In 12-inch non-stick skillet, heat oil and margarine over medium-high heat. Add half of pheasant pieces. Cook for 10 to 12 minutes, or until meat is browned, turning occasionally. Transfer pheasant pieces to 13 × 9-inch baking dish. Repeat with remaining pheasant pieces.

In medium mixing bowl, combine sauce ingredients. Pour sauce over pheasant pieces. Cover dish with foil. Bake for 1 to 1½ hours, or until meat is tender and juices run clear.

Per Serving: Calories: 573 • Protein: 44 g. • Carbohydrate: 41 g. • Fat: 25 g.
• Cholesterol: N/A • Sodium: 1143 mg.
Exchanges: 1 starch, 5 medium-fat meat, 2¾ vegetable, ¾ fruit, ¼ fat

Pineapple Barbecued Pheasant

Julie Mertz – Dakota Hunting Farms, Hecla, South Dakota

1 dressed pheasant or substitute (1½ to 2¼ lbs.), cut up, skin removed
1 can (8 oz.) crushed pineapple in juice, undrained
1 cup barbecue sauce
1 tablespoon cornstarch

3 to 4 servings

Arrange pheasant pieces in 13 × 9-inch baking dish. In small mixing bowl, combine remaining ingredients. Pour over pheasant pieces. Cover with plastic wrap. Chill 4 to 6 hours, turning over once or twice.

Heat oven to 300°F. Remove and discard plastic wrap. Cover dish with foil. Bake for 1 to 1½ hours, or until meat is tender and juices run clear.

Per Serving: Calories: 421 • Protein: 43 g.
• Carbohydrate: 19 g. • Fat: 18 g.
• Cholesterol: N/A • Sodium: 584 mg.
Exchanges: 5½ lean meat, 1¼ vegetable, ¾ fruit, ½ fat

Mary Ingall's Baked Pheasant with Grapes ↑

Bob Schranck – Golden Valley, Minnesota

¼ cup all-purpose flour
¼ teaspoon salt
¼ teaspoon pepper
2 dressed pheasants or substitute (1½ to 2¼ lbs. each), cut up, skin removed
3 tablespoons margarine or butter
3 tablespoons olive oil
1½ cups chopped onions
1 can (10¾ oz.) condensed cream of mushroom soup
1 cup milk
½ cup sour cream
2 cups halved seedless red and green grapes

6 to 8 servings

Heat oven to 350°F. In shallow dish, combine flour, salt and pepper. Dredge pheasant pieces in flour mixture to coat. In 12-inch nonstick skillet, heat margarine and oil over medium-high heat. Add half of pheasant pieces. Cook for 10 to 12 minutes, or until meat is browned, turning occasionally. Transfer pheasant pieces to 13 × 9-inch baking dish. Repeat with remaining pheasant pieces. Set aside.

In same skillet, cook onions over medium heat for 4 to 6 minutes, or until tender, stirring occasionally. Stir in soup and milk. Cook for 1 to 2 minutes, or until mixture is smooth, stirring constantly. Pour sauce over pheasant pieces. Cover dish with foil. Bake for 1½ to 2 hours, or until meat is tender and juices run clear.

In small mixing bowl, combine sour cream and small amount of hot sauce from baking dish. Stir sour cream mixture into sauce in baking dish. Sprinkle with grapes. Re-cover. Bake for 45 minutes to 1 hour, or until sauce is hot and bubbly. Serve with hot cooked wild rice, if desired.

Per Serving: Calories: 550 • Protein: 45 g. • Carbohydrate: 16 g. • Fat: 33 g.
• Cholesterol: N/A • Sodium: 524 mg.
Exchanges: ½ starch, 6 medium-fat meat, ½ vegetable, ½ fruit, ½ fat

Poached Pheasant Salad

William D. Gregoire – Minneapolis, Minnesota

1   dressed pheasant or substitute
    (1½ to 2¼ lbs.), cut up, skin on
6   cups water
1   small onion, cut into 4 wedges
½   cup sliced carrot
½   cup sliced celery
¼   teaspoon dried thyme leaves
1   bay leaf
6   whole peppercorns
4   cups chopped romaine lettuce
2   cups chopped curly endive
1   cup roasted red pepper strips
    (1 × ¼-inch strips)
1   cup seeded chopped tomatoes
1   small bulb fresh fennel, cut into
    ½-inch strips (about ¼ cup)
¼   cup sliced pitted ripe olives

DRESSING:
⅓   cup olive oil
3   tablespoons balsamic vinegar
1   tablespoon snipped fresh basil
    leaves
1   teaspoon Dijon mustard
½   teaspoon freshly ground pepper
¼   teaspoon salt

6 to 8 servings

In 6-quart Dutch oven or stockpot, combine pheasant pieces, water, onion, carrot, celery, thyme, bay leaf and peppercorns. Bring to a boil over medium-high heat. Reduce heat to low. Simmer for 45 minutes to 1 hour, or until meat is tender. Remove from heat. Remove pheasant pieces from broth. Cool slightly. Remove meat from bones. Discard bones and skin. Cut meat into ¾-inch pieces. Strain and reserve broth for future use.

In large salad bowl or mixing bowl, combine meat, romaine, endive, pepper strips, tomatoes, fennel and olives. Set aside. In small mixing bowl, combine dressing ingredients. Pour dressing over salad. Toss to coat.

Per Serving: Calories: 210 • Protein: 20 g.
• Carbohydrate: 4 g. • Fat: 13 g.
• Cholesterol: N/A • Sodium: 164 mg.
Exchanges: 2½ lean meat, 1 vegetable, 1 fat

Pheasant Pie

Donna Tonelli – Lake Andes, South Dakota

2 lbs. pheasant pieces or
     substitute, skin on
10 cups water
2 stalks celery, cut into 3-inch
     lengths
1 small onion, quartered
½ teaspoon whole peppercorns
1 bay leaf

CRUST:
2 cups all-purpose flour
1 teaspoon salt
¾ cup vegetable shortening or lard
1 tablespoon vinegar
2 to 3 tablespoons cold water

1 cup frozen mixed vegetables
2 tablespoons cornstarch
1 teaspoon dried basil leaves
1 teaspoon seasoned salt
½ teaspoon freshly ground pepper

6 servings

In 6-quart Dutch oven or stockpot, combine pheasant pieces, 10 cups water, the celery, onion, peppercorns and bay leaf. Bring to a boil over medium-high heat. Reduce heat to low. Cover. Simmer for 45 minutes to 1 hour, or until meat is tender. Cool completely.

Heat oven to 350°F. In small mixing bowl, combine flour and salt. Using pastry blender, cut in shortening until particles resemble coarse crumbs. Add vinegar. Mix well. Sprinkle with water, 1 tablespoon at a time, mixing with fork until particles are moistened and cling together. Shape dough into ball. Cover bowl with plastic wrap. Chill 15 minutes. Divide dough in half. On lightly floured surface, roll half of dough into 12-inch circle. Fit circle into 9-inch pie plate. Set aside.

Remove pheasant pieces from broth. Remove meat from bones. Discard bones and skin. Shred meat. Strain enough broth to equal 2 cups. Set aside. Strain and reserve remaining broth for future use. Spoon meat into prepared pie plate. Spread mixed vegetables evenly over meat. Set aside.

In 1-quart saucepan, combine cornstarch, basil, seasoned salt and ground pepper. Blend in 2 cups strained broth. Bring to a boil over medium heat. Cook for 1 to 2 minutes, or until sauce is thickened and translucent, stirring constantly. Pour sauce over vegetables and meat.

On lightly floured surface, roll remaining dough into 11-inch circle. Cut vents in circle with 1-inch cookie cutters or slit with sharp knife. Place circle over filling. Roll edges of bottom and top crusts together. Flute edges or press together with tines of fork to seal. Bake for 50 minutes to 1 hour, or until crust is deep golden brown.

Per Serving: Calories: 562 • Protein: 32 g. • Carbohydrate: 39 g. • Fat: 30 g.
• Cholesterol: N/A • Sodium: 633 mg.
Exchanges: 2¼ starch, 3½ lean meat, 4 fat

Cranberry Salsa →

Keith Sutton – Benton, Arkansas

4 teaspoons grated orange peel
2 large seedless oranges, peeled and coarsely chopped (about 2 cups)
2 cups fresh or frozen cranberries, chopped
¼ cup finely chopped onion
¼ cup vegetable oil
1 jalapeño pepper, seeded and finely chopped (about 1 tablespoon)
1 tablespoon grated fresh gingerroot
1 tablespoon snipped fresh cilantro leaves
1 tablespoon sugar
½ teaspoon salt

8 servings

In medium nonmetallic mixing bowl, combine all ingredients. Cover with plastic wrap. Refrigerate 8 hours or overnight. Serve over leftover sliced wild turkey breast or as a condiment with grilled pheasant, quail or chukar.

Per Serving: Calories: 105 • Protein: 1 g.
• Carbohydrate: 11 g. • Fat: 7 g.
• Cholesterol: 0 mg. • Sodium: 137 mg.
Exchanges: ⅔ fruit, 1⅓ fat

Quail à la Covey

Donald C. McCarter – The Covey, Barwick, Georgia

¼ cup plus 1 tablespoon margarine or butter, divided
12 boneless skinless whole quail breasts (1½ oz. each), split in half
1 lb. fresh medium shrimp, shelled and deveined
8 oz. fresh mushrooms, cut into quarters (3 cups)
3 tablespoons all-purpose flour
1 cup milk
½ cup white port wine
¼ teaspoon celery salt
¼ teaspoon garlic powder
¼ teaspoon white pepper

4 to 6 servings

In 12-inch nonstick skillet, melt ¼ cup margarine over medium heat. Add breast halves. Cook for 5 to 7 minutes, or until meat is browned, turning over once. Add shrimp and mushrooms. Cook for 5 to 7 minutes, or until shrimp are firm and opaque and mushrooms are tender, stirring constantly. Using slotted spoon, remove breast halves, shrimp and mushrooms from skillet. Cover to keep warm. Set aside.

In same skillet, melt remaining 1 tablespoon margarine over low heat. Stir in flour. Cook for 8 to 10 minutes, or until deep golden brown, stirring frequently. Gradually blend in milk. Cook for 2 to 4 minutes, or until sauce thickens and bubbles, stirring constantly. Return quail mixture to skillet. Add remaining ingredients. Cook over medium heat for 4 to 6 minutes, or until mixture is thickened and flavors are blended, stirring constantly. Serve over toast points, biscuits or hot cooked rice, if desired.

Per Serving: Calories: 324 • Protein: 32 g. • Carbohydrate: 10 g. • Fat: 14 g.
• Cholesterol: 99 mg. • Sodium: 294 mg.
Exchanges: ½ starch, 4½ lean meat, ½ vegetable, ¼ fat

Woodcock Supreme

"Some upland hunters don't enjoy eating woodcock because the meat can taste like liver. This recipe eliminates the liver taste while adding colorful cooking."
  John O. Cartier – Ludington, Michigan

  2 tablespoons margarine or butter
  4 boneless skinless whole woodcock breasts (2 to 3 oz. each), split in half
  1 small green pepper, thinly sliced
  1 cup finely chopped onions
  ½ cup sliced fresh morel mushrooms
  ½ cup chicken broth
  ¼ cup dry white wine
  3 tablespoons red currant jelly
  1 tablespoon cornstarch mixed with 1 tablespoon water
  ¼ teaspoon salt

2 servings

In 10-inch nonstick skillet, melt margarine over medium heat. Add breast halves. Cook for 4 to 6 minutes, or just until meat is browned, turning over once. Add pepper, onions and mushrooms. Cook for 4 to 5 minutes, or until vegetables are tender-crisp, stirring occasionally.

Add remaining ingredients. Cook over medium heat for 3 to 4 minutes, or until jelly melts and mixture is thickened and translucent, stirring frequently. Serve over hot cooked white or wild rice, if desired.

Nutritional information not available.

Savory Chukar

Sylvia G. Bashline – Spruce Creek, Pennsylvania

  2 tablespoons vegetable oil
  2 tablespoons margarine or butter
  2 to 3 lbs. boneless skinless chukar breasts or substitute, cut into 1-inch pieces
  ½ teaspoon salt
  ¼ teaspoon pepper
  ⅛ teaspoon dried summer savory
  ¾ cup whipping cream
  3 tablespoons Madeira wine
  ¼ teaspoon crushed red pepper flakes

10 servings

In 10-inch nonstick skillet, heat oil and margarine over medium heat. Add chukar pieces, salt, pepper and summer savory. Cook for 8 to 10 minutes, or just until meat is browned, stirring frequently. Stir in cream, wine and pepper flakes. Reduce heat to low. Cook for 8 to 10 minutes, or until hot, stirring occasionally. Serve over hot buttered rice and garnish with snipped fresh parsley, if desired.

Per Serving: Calories: 265 • Protein: 28 g. • Carbohydrate: 1 g. • Fat: 15 g.
• Cholesterol: N/A • Sodium: 181 mg.
Exchanges: 4 lean meat, ¾ fat

Sharptail Paprika

"Although sharptail breast is dark, the meat pleasantly surprises people with its mild, beeflike flavor."
Charles E. Carpenter – Wellsville, Utah

¼ cup all-purpose flour
¼ cup sweet Hungarian paprika, divided
1 teaspoon dried marjoram leaves
1 teaspoon salt
¼ teaspoon pepper
1½ lbs. boneless skinless sharptail grouse breasts or substitute, cut into 1-inch pieces
3 tablespoons olive oil
3 tablespoons margarine or butter
1 cup chopped onions
2 cloves garlic, minced
½ cup dry red wine
½ cup beef broth
½ cup orange juice
1 to 2 teaspoons Dijon mustard (optional)
¼ cup sour cream
Hot cooked egg noodles, tossed in butter with poppy seed

6 servings

In large plastic food-storage bag, combine flour, 1 tablespoon paprika, the marjoram, salt and pepper. Add grouse pieces. Shake to coat. In 12-inch nonstick skillet, heat oil and margarine over medium heat. Add grouse pieces, onions and garlic. Cook for 5 to 7 minutes, or until meat is browned, stirring frequently.

Stir in remaining 3 tablespoons paprika, the wine and broth. Reduce heat to medium-low. Simmer for 20 to 30 minutes, or until sauce is thickened, stirring occasionally.

Increase heat to medium. Stir in juice and mustard. Simmer for 8 to 10 minutes, or until sauce is thickened, stirring occasionally. Remove from heat. Stir in sour cream. Serve over noodles. Garnish with snipped fresh parsley, if desired.

Nutritional information not available.

Foolproof Pheasant & Wild Rice ↑

Bob Schranck – Golden Valley, Minnesota

¼ cup margarine or butter
3 boneless skinless whole pheasant breasts or substitute (8 oz. each), cut into ¾-inch pieces
1 cup chopped onions
1 can (10¾ oz.) condensed cream of mushroom soup
1 can (10¾ oz.) condensed cream of chicken soup
2 jars (4½ oz. each) button or sliced mushrooms, drained
1 can (8 oz.) sliced water chestnuts, rinsed and drained
1 cup water
1 cup uncooked wild rice, rinsed and drained
½ cup cooking sherry
¼ to ½ teaspoon coarsely ground pepper
½ cup slivered almonds, toasted (optional)

8 servings

Heat oven to 325°F. In 10-inch nonstick skillet, melt margarine over medium-high heat. Add pheasant pieces and onions. Cook for 10 to 12 minutes, or until meat is browned, stirring occasionally.

In 3-quart casserole, combine pheasant mixture and remaining ingredients, except almonds. Cover. Bake for 2 to 2½ hours, or until rice is tender and kernels are open, stirring once during baking. Sprinkle almonds evenly over top.

Per Serving: Calories: 342 • Protein: 26 g. • Carbohydrate: 28 g. • Fat: 14 g.
• Cholesterol: N/A • Sodium: 874 mg.
Exchanges: 1⅔ starch, 3 lean meat, ¾ vegetable, ¾ fat

Festive Pheasant Stir-fry

Joyce Ingalls – Bryant, South Dakota

1 can (16 oz.) pineapple chunks
  or tidbits in juice, drained·
  (reserve ¾ cup juice)
¼ cup plus 1 tablespoon soy sauce
¼ cup packed brown sugar
¼ cup white vinegar
3 tablespoons cornstarch
1 tablespoon catsup
1 teaspoon seasoned salt
½ teaspoon freshly ground pepper
3 boneless skinless whole pheasant
  breasts or substitute (8 oz. each),
  cut into 1-inch pieces
3 tablespoons olive oil, divided
¼ cup coarsely chopped walnuts
1 medium green pepper, cut into
  2 × ¼-inch strips
4 oz. fresh mushrooms, sliced
  (1½ cups)
2 tablespoons chopped onion
¼ to ½ teaspoon crushed red
  pepper flakes (optional)

6 servings

In medium nonmetallic mixing bowl, combine pineapple juice, the soy sauce, brown sugar, vinegar, cornstarch, catsup, salt and pepper. Add pheasant pieces. Stir to coat. Cover with plastic wrap. Refrigerate 5 hours or overnight. Refrigerate pineapple chunks.

In wok or 12-inch nonstick skillet, heat 2 tablespoons oil over medium-high heat. Add walnuts. Cook for 2 to 3 minutes, or just until nuts begin to brown, stirring frequently. Using slotted spoon, remove nuts from skillet. Set aside.

To same skillet, add pepper strips, mushrooms and onion. Cook for 3 to 4 minutes, or until vegetables are tender-crisp, stirring frequently. Remove vegetables from skillet. Set aside.

In same skillet, heat remaining 1 tablespoon oil over medium-high heat. Drain and reserve marinade from pheasant pieces. Add pheasant pieces to skillet. Cook for 6 to 7 minutes, or until meat is browned, stirring frequently.

Add reserved marinade. Cook for 2 to 3 minutes, or until mixture is thickened and translucent, stirring constantly. Add pineapple and pepper flakes. Return walnuts and vegetable mixture to skillet. Cook for 3 to 4 minutes, or until mixture is hot, stirring frequently. Serve with hot cooked white rice, if desired.

Per Serving: Calories: 357 • Protein: 30 g. • Carbohydrate: 30 g. • Fat: 14 g.
• Cholesterol: N/A • Sodium: 931 mg.
Exchanges: 4 lean meat, 1 vegetable, 1⅔ fruit, ⅓ fat

Game Bird Sausage-stuffed Pizza

The Hunting & Fishing Library®

¼ cup olive oil, divided
½ lb. uncooked bulk Game Bird
    Sausage (page 116), crumbled
½ medium yellow, green, or red
    pepper, cut into 2 × ¼-inch strips
½ cup seeded chopped tomato
⅓ cup sliced pimiento-stuffed
    green olives
2 tablespoons tomato paste
½ teaspoon Italian seasoning
1 pkg. (16 oz.) hot roll mix
1 cup hot water (120° to 130°F)
1 egg
½ cup shredded mozzarella or
    Monterey Jack cheese
1 clove garlic, minced
¼ teaspoon crushed red pepper
    flakes

6 servings

Lightly grease pizza pan or baking sheet. Set aside. In 10-inch nonstick skillet, heat 1 tablespoon oil over medium heat. Add sausage. Cook for 5 to 7 minutes, or until meat is golden brown, stirring occasionally. Add pepper strips, tomato, olives, tomato paste and Italian seasoning. Cook for 3 to 4 minutes, or until pepper strips are tender-crisp, stirring frequently. Remove from heat. Cover to keep warm. Set filling aside.

In large mixing bowl, combine hot roll mix, water, egg and 2 tablespoons of remaining oil. Turn dough out onto lightly floured surface. Shape into ball. Knead for 5 to 7 minutes, or until smooth. Cover dough with bowl. Let rest for 5 minutes. Divide dough in half.

On lightly floured surface, roll half of dough into 10-inch circle. Place circle on prepared pan. Spoon filling onto circle, spreading filling to within ½ inch of edge. Sprinkle cheese evenly over filling. On lightly floured surface, roll remaining dough into 10-inch circle. Fit second circle over filling, pressing edges to seal. Cover pizza with light cloth. Let rise in warm place for 20 to 30 minutes, or until almost double in size.

Heat oven to 350°F. Using end of wooden spoon, make indentations in dough, about 1 inch apart. Brush surface of pizza with remaining 1 table-spoon oil. Sprinkle garlic and red pepper flakes evenly over surface. Bake for 25 to 30 minutes, or until pizza is golden brown. Serve in wedges.

Per Serving: Calories: 488 • Protein: 15 g. • Carbohydrate: 57 g. • Fat: 23 g.
• Cholesterol: 74 mg. • Sodium: 849 mg.
Exchanges: 3½ starch, 1 high-fat meat, 3 fat

Prairie Pheasant Bake

Colleen J. Schlosser – Edgeley, North Dakota

¼ cup all-purpose flour
¼ teaspoon celery salt
¼ teaspoon pepper
3 boneless skinless whole pheasant breasts or
   substitute (8 oz. each), cut into 1-inch strips
2 tablespoons vegetable oil
¼ cup margarine or butter
8 oz. fresh mushrooms, thinly sliced (3 cups)
2 cups thinly sliced celery
1 cup chopped red or green pepper
1 cup chopped onions
2 tablespoons slivered almonds (optional)

Sauce:
2 tablespoons margarine or butter
½ cup all-purpose flour
1 tablespoon dried parsley flakes
½ teaspoon caraway seeds, slightly crushed
½ teaspoon salt
¼ teaspoon dried dill weed
1 can (14½ oz.) chicken broth
½ cup water

½ cup sour cream

6 to 8 servings

Heat oven to 300°F. In large plastic food-storage bag, combine ¼ cup flour, the celery salt and pepper. Add pheasant strips. Shake to coat.

In 12-inch nonstick skillet, heat oil over medium-high heat. Add pheasant strips. Cook for 8 to 10 minutes, or until meat is golden brown, turning over frequently. Transfer pheasant strips to 3-quart casserole. Set aside.

In same skillet, melt ¼ cup margarine over medium heat. Add mushrooms, celery, red pepper and onions. Cook for 3 to 5 minutes, or until vegetables are tender-crisp, stirring occasionally. Stir in almonds. Spoon vegetable mixture over pheasant.

In same skillet, melt 2 tablespoons margarine over medium heat. Stir in flour, parsley, caraway, salt and dill weed. Blend in broth and water. Bring to a boil over medium-high heat. Cook for 2 to 4 minutes, or until sauce thickens and bubbles, stirring constantly.

Pour sauce over pheasant mixture. Cover. Bake for 50 minutes to 1 hour, or until hot and bubbly. Stir in sour cream. Serve over hot cooked wild rice, if desired.

Per Serving: Calories: 323 • Protein: 24 g. • Carbohydrate: 15 g.
• Fat: 18 g. • Cholesterol: N/A • Sodium: 544 mg.
Exchanges: ⅔ starch, 3 lean meat, 1 vegetable, 2 fat

Pheasant Hot Dish

Joyce Ingalls – Ingalls Prairie Wildfowl
Hunts, Bryant, South Dakota

    6 oz. uncooked mini lasagna
         noodles (4 cups)
    3½ cups cut-up cooked pheasant
         or substitute (about 1 lb.)
    1¼ cups milk
    1 can (10¾ oz.) condensed
         cream of mushroom soup
    1 cup shredded pasteurized
         process cheese loaf
    1 can (4 oz.) sliced mushrooms,
         drained
    1 clove garlic, minced
    1 teaspoon instant chicken
         bouillon granules
    ½ teaspoon pepper
    ½ teaspoon dried thyme leaves
    1 tablespoon margarine or butter
    1 cup thinly sliced celery
    ½ cup chopped green pepper
    ½ cup chopped red pepper
    ½ cup chopped onion
    1 cup crushed potato chips

6 to 8 servings

Heat oven to 350°F. Spray 3-quart casserole with nonstick vegetable cooking spray. Set aside. Prepare noodles as directed on package. Rinse and drain. In large mixing bowl, combine noodles, pheasant pieces, milk, soup, cheese, mushrooms, garlic, bouillon, pepper and thyme. Set aside.

In 10-inch nonstick skillet, melt margarine over medium heat. Add celery, peppers and onion. Cook for 3 to 5 minutes, or until vegetables are tender-crisp, stirring occasionally. Add to pheasant mixture.

Spoon pheasant mixture into prepared casserole. Sprinkle top evenly with potato chips. Bake for 30 to 35 minutes, or until mixture is hot and bubbly and topping is golden brown.

Per Serving: Calories: 345 • Protein: 26 g.
• Carbohydrate: 29 g. • Fat: 14 g.
• Cholesterol: N/A • Sodium: 792 mg.
Exchanges: 1½ starch, 2¾ lean meat,
1 vegetable, 1¼ fat

Partridge & Hazelnut Salad ↑

Thomas K. Squier – Aberdeen, North Carolina

    2 cups cut-up cooked Hungarian
         partridge or substitute (about
         10 oz.)
    ½ cup coarsely chopped hazelnuts,
         toasted, divided
    1 cup thinly sliced celery
    ½ cup halved seedless green grapes
    ½ cup halved seedless red grapes
    ½ cup mayonnaise or salad
         dressing
    ¼ cup plain nonfat or low-fat
         yogurt
    1 tablespoon honey
    1 tablespoon lemon juice
    ½ teaspoon ground ginger
    ⅛ teaspoon salt

4 servings

In large mixing bowl, combine partridge pieces, ¼ cup hazelnuts, the celery and grapes. Set aside. In small mixing bowl, combine remaining ingredients, except remaining hazelnuts. Spoon mayonnaise mixture over partridge mixture. Toss to coat. Serve salad on lettuce-lined plates, if desired. Sprinkle servings evenly with remaining ¼ cup hazelnuts.

Per Serving: Calories: 474 • Protein: 27 g. • Carbohydrate: 15 g. • Fat: 35 g.
• Cholesterol: N/A • Sodium: 302 mg.
Exchanges: 4 medium-fat meat, 1 fruit, 3 fat

Waterfowl

← Fruited Roast Goose

Donna Tonelli – Lake Andes, South Dakota

1 whole dressed Canada goose
(6 to 8 lbs.), skin on
½ teaspoon salt
½ teaspoon pepper
1 medium seedless orange, cut
into 8 wedges
1 medium red cooking apple,
cored and cut into 8 wedges
1 can (16 oz.) sliced peaches in
syrup, drained (reserve ½ cup
syrup)
1 tablespoon vegetable oil
1¾ cups beef broth
2 tablespoons cornstarch mixed
with 2 tablespoons water
1 tablespoon soy sauce

6 servings

Heat oven to 350°F. Sprinkle cavity of goose with salt and pepper. Stuff goose loosely with orange, apple and peach slices. Secure legs with string. Tuck wing tips behind back. Brush goose with oil. Place goose breast-side-up on rack in roasting pan. Pour broth and reserved peach syrup around goose. Bake for 20 to 25 minutes per pound, or until legs move freely and juices run clear, basting occasionally with pan drippings. Transfer goose to warm platter. Let stand, tented with foil, for 10 to 15 minutes.

Meanwhile, strain drippings from bottom of roasting pan. Skim and discard fat from drippings. In 1-quart saucepan, combine 2 cups drippings, the cornstarch mixture and soy sauce. Cook over medium heat for 5 to 7 minutes, or until sauce thickens and bubbles, stirring constantly. Serve sauce with carved goose.

Per Serving: Calories: 770 • Protein: 55 g.
• Carbohydrate: 26 g. • Fat: 50 g.
• Cholesterol: 194 mg. • Sodium: 749 mg.
Exchanges: 8 medium-fat meat, 1⅔ fruit, 2 fat

Maryland Wild Goose ↑

W. Beirne Keefer – Clearwater, Florida

1 cup margarine or butter
2 cups thinly sliced celery
½ cup chopped onion
4 cups unseasoned dry bread
crumbs
2 medium red cooking apples,
cored and cut into 1-inch chunks
3 hard-cooked eggs, chopped
1 cup snipped fresh parsley

½ teaspoon salt
¼ teaspoon pepper
¼ teaspoon dried basil leaves
¼ teaspoon poultry seasoning
⅛ teaspoon dried thyme leaves
Dash cayenne
1 whole dressed wild goose
(4 to 6 lbs.), skin on
4 slices bacon

4 to 6 servings

Heat oven to 325°F. In 10-inch nonstick skillet, melt margarine over medium heat. Add celery and onion. Cook for 3 to 4 minutes, or until vegetables are tender, stirring occasionally. Remove from heat.

In large mixing bowl, combine celery mixture, bread crumbs, apples, eggs, parsley, salt, pepper, basil, poultry seasoning, thyme and cayenne.

Spoon stuffing into cavity of goose. (Extra stuffing may be wrapped in foil and baked separately.) Secure legs with string. Tuck wing tips behind back. Place goose breast-side-up on rack in roasting pan. Place bacon slices across breast. Bake for 20 to 25 minutes per pound, or until legs move freely and juices run clear, basting occasionally with pan drippings.

Note: If substituting domestic goose, omit bacon and skim and discard excess fat from drippings during baking.

Per Serving: Calories: 1180 • Protein: 58 g. • Carbohydrate: 63 g. • Fat: 76 g.
• Cholesterol: 268 mg. • Sodium: 1354 mg.
Exchanges: 3½ starch, 6½ medium-fat meat, ½ fruit, 8½ fat

Mallards with Wild Rice

Col. Lyle B. Otto – Gig Harbor, Washington

2 whole dressed mallards or
   substitute (1¼ to 1½ lbs. each),
   skin on
1 teaspoon salt, divided
½ teaspoon pepper, divided
1 small red cooking apple, cored
   and cut into 8 wedges
1 small onion, cut into 6 wedges
2 stalks celery, cut into 1-inch
   lengths
1 medium seedless orange, cut
   into 6 wedges
½ cup dry red wine
½ cup water
1 tablespoon vegetable oil
1 pkg. (5 oz.) brown and wild rice
   with mushrooms
½ teaspoon grated orange peel

4 servings

Heat oven to 450°F. Sprinkle cavities of ducks evenly with ½ teaspoon salt and ¼ teaspoon pepper. Stuff ducks evenly with apple, onion and celery. Secure legs with string. Tuck wing tips behind back. Place ducks breast-side-up in 12 × 8-inch baking dish. Arrange orange wedges around ducks. Pour wine and water around ducks. Brush ducks evenly with oil. Sprinkle evenly with remaining ½ teaspoon salt and ¼ teaspoon pepper. Bake for 25 to 30 minutes, or until skin is golden brown.

Reduce heat to 325°F. Cover ducks with foil. Bake for 1½ to 2 hours longer, or until meat is desired doneness. Meanwhile, prepare rice as directed on package. Stir peel into rice before serving. Remove and discard stuffing from ducks before serving.

Per Serving: Calories: 606 • Protein: 27 g.
• Carbohydrate: 34 g. • Fat: 41 g.
• Cholesterol: 108 mg. • Sodium: 1152 mg.
Exchanges: 2 starch, 3 medium-fat meat,
¼ fruit, 5 fat

Bahama Roast Mallard ↑

Donna and Ken White – Independence, Missouri

4 whole dressed mallards or
   substitute (1¼ to 1½ lbs. each),
   skin on
¼ cup lime juice
2 tablespoons orange marmalade
4 cloves garlic, minced
1 tablespoon water

1 teaspoon rum
1 teaspoon seasoned salt
1 medium seedless orange,
   peeled and quartered
4 cloves garlic
12 peppercorns

8 servings

Place ducks breast-side-up in 15½ x 10½-inch jelly roll pan or large roasting pan. Set aside. In small mixing bowl, combine juice, marmalade, minced garlic, water and rum. Brush ducks evenly with mixture. Cover with plastic wrap. Chill 6 to 8 hours.

Heat oven to 300°F. Remove ducks from pan. Drain and reserve marmalade mixture. Sprinkle ¼ teaspoon salt over each duck. Place 1 orange quarter, 1 garlic clove and 3 peppercorns in cavity of each duck.

Arrange ducks breast-side-up in same jelly roll pan. Bake for 1½ to 2 hours, or until meat is desired doneness, brushing several times with reserved marmalade mixture. Serve with hot cooked rice and fried plantains, if desired.

NOTE: For crisper skin, increase oven temperature to 400°F during last 15 minutes of baking.

Per Serving: Calories: 428 • Protein: 23 g. • Carbohydrate: 7 g. • Fat: 34 g.
• Cholesterol: 100 mg. • Sodium: 231 mg.
Exchanges: 3¼ high-fat meat, ½ fruit, 1½ fat

Crisp Apple-glazed Duck

Ferne Holmes – Phoenix, Arizona

1 whole dressed mallard or substitute
   (1¼ to 1½ lbs.), skin on
1 large red cooking apple, cored
   and cut into 1-inch chunks
1 cup boiling water
1 teaspoon instant chicken bouillon
   granules

APPLE GLAZE:

½ cup apple jelly
2 tablespoons apple juice or dry
   white wine

2 servings

Heat oven to 375°F. Stuff duck loosely with apple. Secure legs with string. Tuck wing tips behind back. Place duck breast-side-up on rack in roasting pan. In small mixing bowl, combine water and bouillon. Stir until bouillon is dissolved. Pour half of bouillon mixture over duck. Bake for 45 minutes, basting occasionally with remaining bouillon mixture.

Meanwhile, in 1-quart saucepan, combine glaze ingredients. Cook over medium heat until jelly is melted. Brush duck with some of glaze. Bake for 10 to 20 minutes, or until meat is desired doneness, basting frequently with some of remaining glaze. Garnish with apple slices and fresh parsley, if desired. Serve any remaining warm glaze with duck.

Per Serving: Calories: 687 • Protein: 23 g. • Carbohydrate: 74 g. • Fat: 34 g.
• Cholesterol: 100 mg. • Sodium: 579 mg.
Exchanges: 3⅓ high-fat meat, 5 fruit, 1½ fat

← Marmalade Goose Breast

William F. Carney – Beverly, Massachusetts

  2 cups milk
 ½ teaspoon white vinegar
  1 boneless skinless whole Canada
      goose breast (about 1 lb.)
 ½ cup dry white wine
 ½ cup apple cider or apple juice
 ⅓ cup frozen orange juice
      concentrate, defrosted
1½ teaspoons grated orange peel
  2 tablespoons orange marmalade

4 servings

In medium mixing bowl, combine milk and vinegar. Add goose breast, turning to coat. Cover with plastic wrap. Refrigerate 8 hours or overnight, turning once or twice.

Drain and discard milk mixture. In second medium mixing bowl, combine wine, cider, concentrate and peel. Add goose breast, turning to coat. Cover with plastic wrap. Chill 4 to 6 hours, turning once or twice.

Heat oven to 425°F. Line 8-inch square baking dish with heavy-duty foil, allowing foil to extend about 10 inches on each side. Drain wine mixture, reserving ¼ cup. Place goose breast in prepared dish. Pour reserved wine mixture over goose. Fold opposite sides of foil together in locked folds. Fold and crimp ends. Bake for 30 to 35 minutes, or until meat is desired doneness.

Fold back foil. Brush marmalade over goose breast. Bake, with foil open, for 5 to 10 minutes, or until meat is browned. Carve breast across grain into thin slices. Serve with hot cooked parsleyed rice, if desired.

Per Serving: Calories: 212 • Protein: 26 g.
• Carbohydrate: 5 g. • Fat: 9 g.
• Cholesterol: 97 mg. • Sodium: 108 mg.
Exchanges: 3½ lean meat, ⅓ fruit

Spicy Sauerkraut Duck

David M. Knotts – Jamestown, Colorado

 ¼ cup vegetable oil
  2 whole dressed wild ducks
      (1¼ to 1½ lbs. each), skin
      removed
  1 jar (32 oz.) sauerkraut, undrained
  1 cup sliced green onions
  1 cup coarsely shredded carrots
 ½ teaspoon freshly ground pepper
 ¼ teaspoon cayenne
  1 large jalapeño pepper, sliced

4 servings

In 6-quart Dutch oven or stockpot, heat oil over medium heat. Add ducks. Cook for 8 to 10 minutes, or until meat is browned, turning occasionally. Remove ducks. Drain and discard oil from Dutch oven. Return ducks to Dutch oven.

Add remaining ingredients, except jalapeño pepper. Stir to combine. Bring to a boil over medium-high heat. Reduce heat to low. Cover. Simmer for 1½ to 2 hours, or until meat is tender.

Remove ducks from sauerkraut mixture. Cool slightly. Remove meat from bones. Discard bones. Cut meat into ¾-inch pieces. Return duck pieces to Dutch oven. Stir in jalapeño pepper. Cook for 5 to 10 minutes, or until jalapeño pepper is tender-crisp.

Per Serving: Calories: 334 • Protein: 34 g. • Carbohydrate: 15 g. • Fat: 16 g.
• Cholesterol: N/A • Sodium: 1603 mg.
Exchanges: 4 lean meat, 3 vegetable, ½ fat

Steve's Grilled Duck →

Gayle Grossman – Little Moran Hunting Club, Staples, Minnesota

- 2 boneless skinless whole wild duck breasts (8 to 12 oz. each), split in half
- 1 medium red cooking apple, cored and cut into ¼-inch slices
- 1 medium onion, sliced
- 1 can (8 oz.) sliced water chestnuts, rinsed and drained
- ½ teaspoon seasoned salt
- ¼ teaspoon freshly ground pepper

4 servings

Prepare grill for barbecuing. Place 1 breast half in center of 12 × 12-inch square of heavy-duty foil. Repeat with remaining breast halves. Arrange apple, onion and water chestnuts evenly over breast halves. Sprinkle evenly with salt and pepper.

Fold opposite sides of foil together in locked folds. Fold and crimp ends. Place packets on cooking grate. Grill for 30 to 45 minutes, or until meat is tender and juices run clear.

Per Serving: Calories: 240 • Protein: 29 g. • Carbohydrate: 16 g. • Fat: 6 g. • Cholesterol: N/A • Sodium: 242 mg. Exchanges: 3¾ lean meat, 2 vegetable, ⅓ fruit

Cross Pepper Ducks

Billy Joe Cross – Brandon, Missisipi

- 2 whole dressed wild ducks (1¼ to 1½ lbs. each), skin on
- 1 tangerine, peeled and cut in half
- 1 medium onion, cut into quarters
- 1 cup chopped celery
- ½ cup dry white wine
- 1 to 2 tablespoons bacon drippings, melted
- 1 teaspoon Cavender's® Greek seasoning
- 2 slices bacon, cut in half crosswise
- ¼ cup hot red pepper jelly, melted

4 servings

Heat oven to 325°F. Line 13 × 9-inch baking dish with heavy-duty foil, allowing foil to extend about 10 inches on each side. Set aside. Place half of tangerine, half of onion quarters, half of celery and ¼ cup wine in each duck cavity. Secure legs with string. Place ducks breast-side-up in prepared dish. Brush ducks with bacon drippings. Sprinkle ducks evenly with seasoning. Place bacon slices across breasts.

Fold long sides of foil together in locked folds. Fold and crimp ends. Bake for 40 to 45 minutes, or until meat is tender. Fold back foil. Brush ducks with jelly. Bake, with foil open, for 30 to 35 minutes, or until skin is lightly browned and juices run clear.

Per Serving: Calories: 580 • Protein: 24 g. • Carbohydrate: 21 g. • Fat: 44 g. • Cholesterol: 111 mg. • Sodium: 208 mg. Exchanges: 3⅓ high-fat meat, 1 vegetable, 1 fruit, 3½ fat

Duck Wellington

Joan N. Cone – Williamsburg, Virginia

2 tablespoons margarine or butter, divided
⅓ cup chopped mushrooms
2 tablespoons sliced green onions
1 tablespoon cognac (optional)
4 oz. liverwurst
1 tablespoon snipped fresh parsley
2 boneless skinless whole wild duck breasts
   (8 to 12 oz. each), split in half,
   pounded to ¼-inch thickness
1 sheet frozen puff pastry, defrosted (half of
   17¼-oz. pkg.)
1 egg beaten with 1 tablespoon water

4 servings

Heat oven to 375°F. In 10-inch nonstick skillet, melt 1 tablespoon margarine over medium heat. Add mushrooms, onions and cognac. Cook for 2 to 3 minutes, or until onions are tender, stirring frequently. In small mixing bowl, combine mushroom mixture, liverwurst and parsley. Set aside.

In same skillet, melt remaining 1 tablespoon margarine over medium heat. Add breast halves. Cook for 8 to 10 minutes, or until meat is browned, turning occasionally. Remove from heat. Cover to keep warm. Set aside. Wrap Duck Wellington as directed below.

Per Serving: Calories: 676 • Protein: 38 g. • Carbohydrate: 29 g. • Fat: 44 g. • Cholesterol: N/A • Sodium: 629 mg.
Exchanges: 2 starch, 4½ lean meat, 4½ fat

How to Wrap Duck Wellington

ROLL pastry sheet to 14-inch square on lightly floured surface. Cut sheet into four 7-inch squares. Place 1 breast half on each square. Spread liverwurst mixture evenly over top of breast halves. Brush edges of pastry with egg mixture.

BRING two sides of pastry together over each breast half. Pinch edges and ends to seal. Place on ungreased baking sheet. Bake for 20 to 25 minutes, or until golden brown.

Seared Duck Breast
with Pan Juices →

*"Any type of jelly works well in place of
the raspberry jam."*
    Teresa Marrone – Minneapolis, Minnesota

 2 boneless whole wild duck breasts
      (8 to 12 oz. each), split in half,
      skin on
¼ teaspoon salt
¼ teaspoon pepper
¾ cup dry sherry
 2 tablespoons raspberry preserves
 2 tablespoons margarine or butter
½ cup chopped onion

4 servings

Sprinkle breast halves evenly with
salt and pepper. Set aside. In small
mixing bowl, combine sherry and
preserves. Set aside. In 10-inch nonstick skillet, melt margarine over
medium heat. Add breast halves.
Cook for 3 minutes. Turn breast
halves over. Add onion. Cook for
2 to 3 minutes, or until meat is
lightly browned.

Pour sherry mixture over breast
halves. Cook for 4 to 8 minutes, or
until meat is desired doneness and
liquid is slightly reduced. To serve,
carve breast halves crosswise into
slices. Fan slices out slightly over
hot cooked pasta, if desired. Top
with onion and pan juices.

Per Serving: Calories: 326 • Protein: 29 g.
• Carbohydrate: 14 g. • Fat: 12 g.
• Cholesterol: N/A • Sodium: 291 mg.
Exchanges: 4 lean meat, ¼ vegetable,
¾ fruit

Duck Piccata

Thomas K. Squier – Aberdeen, North Carolina

⅓ cup all-purpose flour
½ teaspoon salt
¼ teaspoon freshly ground pepper
 2 boneless skinless whole wild
      duck breasts (8 to 12 oz. each),
      split in half, pounded to ¼-inch
      thickness
 3 tablespoons butter
¼ cup dry white wine
 3 tablespoons fresh lemon juice
 2 tablespoons capers, drained

4 servings

In shallow dish, combine flour, salt and pepper. Dredge breast halves in
flour mixture to coat. In 12-inch nonstick skillet, melt butter over medium
heat. Add breast halves. Cook for 8 to 10 minutes, or until meat is browned,
turning occasionally. Transfer breast halves to warm platter. Cover to keep
warm. Set aside.

To same skillet, add wine and juice. Stir to loosen browned bits in skillet.
Cook for 3 to 5 minutes, or until sauce is reduced slightly. Remove from
heat. Stir in capers. Spoon sauce over breast halves. Garnish with fresh
lemon slices, if desired.

Per Serving: Calories: 301 • Protein: 29 g. • Carbohydrate: 9 g. • Fat: 15 g.
• Cholesterol: N/A • Sodium: 553 mg.
Exchanges: ⅔ starch, 4 lean meat, ½ fat

Oriental Barbecued Black Duck

Teresa Marrone – Minneapolis, Minnesota

2   dressed black ducks (1¼ to
      1½ lbs. each), cut up, skin on
1   whole fresh pineapple (3½ to
      4 lbs.), peeled, cored and cut
      lengthwise into 8 wedges
8   green onions, cut into 6-inch
      lengths
¼   cup dry sherry
¼   cup hoisin sauce
3   tablespoons Chinese plum sauce
3   tablespoons fresh lemon juice
2   tablespoons Chinese black bean
      sauce
3   cloves garlic
1   cube peeled fresh gingerroot
      (1-inch cube)

4 servings

In 13 × 9-inch baking dish, arrange duck pieces, pineapple and onions. Set aside. In food processor or blender, combine remaining ingredients. Process just until garlic and ginger are finely chopped. Pour mixture over duck pieces, turning to coat. Cover with plastic wrap. Chill 4 to 6 hours.

Prepare grill for barbecuing. Spray cooking grate with nonstick vegetable cooking spray. Arrange duck pieces on center of prepared grate. Grill, partially covered, for 20 to 30 minutes, or until meat is desired doneness, turning duck pieces twice. Place duck pieces on edges of grate to keep warm.

Arrange pineapple and onions on center of grate. Grill, covered, for 5 to 10 minutes, or until lightly browned, turning over once. Serve with hot cooked Basmati rice or white rice, if desired.

Per Serving: Calories: 644 • Protein: 28 g.
• Carbohydrate: 42 g. • Fat: 40 g.
• Cholesterol: 113 mg. • Sodium: 657 mg.
Exchanges: 4 high-fat meat, 2¾ fruit,
1½ fat

Collin's Fricasseed Duck

Bob Schranck – Golden Valley, Minnesota

⅓ cup all-purpose flour
1 teaspoon salt
½ teaspoon freshly ground pepper
2 dressed wild ducks (1¼ to 1½ lbs. each), skin and bones removed, cut into 1-inch pieces
¼ cup margarine or butter
1 cup finely chopped onions
1 cup small fresh mushroom caps
1 small green pepper, thinly sliced into rings
1 cup water
½ cup Burgundy wine
2 bay leaves
8 oz. uncooked egg noodles

4 servings

In large plastic food-storage bag, combine flour, salt and pepper. Add duck pieces. Shake to coat. In 12-inch nonstick skillet, melt margarine over medium-high heat. Add duck pieces, onions, mushrooms and pepper rings. Cook for 5 to 7 minutes, or until meat is browned, stirring occasionally.

Add water, wine and bay leaves. Bring to a boil. Reduce heat to low. Simmer for 40 to 45 minutes, or until meat is tender, stirring occasionally. Remove and discard bay leaves. Meanwhile, prepare noodles as directed on package. Rinse and drain. Serve mixture over noodles.

Per Serving: Calories: 577 • Protein: 41 g. • Carbohydrate: 55 g. • Fat: 21 g. • Cholesterol: N/A • Sodium: 789 mg.
Exchanges: 1½ starch, 4¼ lean meat, 1 vegetable, 1⅓ fat

Sweet & Sour Duck

Louis Bignami – Moscow, Idaho

1 tablespoon dry sherry
2 teaspoons soy sauce
¼ teaspoon salt
1 boneless skinless whole wild
　 duck breast (8 to 12 oz.), cut
　 into 1-inch pieces
¼ cup chicken broth
¼ cup cider vinegar
¼ cup packed brown sugar
3 tablespoons catsup
1 teaspoon grated lemon peel
1 can (8 oz.) pineapple chunks
　 in juice, drained (reserve
　 1 tablespoon juice)
2 eggs
1 cup all-purpose flour, divided
½ teaspoon baking powder
⅓ cup vegetable oil
1 clove garlic, minced
1 teaspoon minced fresh
　 gingerroot
2 cups red and green pepper
　 chunks (1-inch chunks)
½ small onion, cut into 1-inch
　 chunks
2 teaspoons cornstarch mixed
　 with 1 tablespoon cold water

4 to 6 servings

In medium mixing bowl, combine sherry, soy sauce and salt. Add duck pieces. Stir to coat. Cover with plastic wrap. Chill 30 minutes. In small mixing bowl, combine broth, vinegar, sugar, catsup, peel and reserved pineapple juice. Set sauce aside.

In shallow dish, lightly beat eggs. Place ½ cup flour on sheet of wax paper. On second sheet of wax paper, combine remaining ½ cup flour and the baking powder. Dredge duck pieces first in plain flour, then dip in eggs, and then dredge in flour mixture to coat. Arrange duck pieces in single layer on wax-paper-lined baking sheet.

In 12-inch nonstick skillet or wok, heat oil over medium-high heat. Add duck pieces. Cook for 3 to 4 minutes, or until meat is lightly browned, stirring frequently. Drain duck pieces on paper-towel-lined plate. Cover to keep warm. Set aside.

In same skillet, cook garlic and gingerroot over medium heat for 30 seconds, stirring constantly. Add sauce, pineapple chunks, peppers and onion. Cook for 2 to 3 minutes, or until vegetables are tender-crisp, stirring constantly. Stir in cornstarch mixture. Cook for 1 to 2 minutes, or until sauce is thickened and translucent, stirring constantly. Remove from heat. Return duck pieces to skillet. Stir to coat. Serve with hot cooked rice, if desired.

Per Serving: Calories: 366 • Protein: 16 g. • Carbohydrate: 38 g. • Fat: 16 g.
• Cholesterol: N/A • Sodium: 434 mg.
Exchanges: 1 starch, 2 lean meat, 1 vegetable, 1 fruit, 2 fat

Mallard Sauté →

William F. Carney – Beverly, Massachusetts

¼ cup all-purpose flour
2 teaspoons garlic powder
2 teaspoons dried tarragon leaves
1 boneless skinless whole mallard
   breast or substitute (8 to 12 oz.),
   cut into 1-inch strips
¼ cup olive oil
1 tablespoon margarine or butter
4 oz. fresh mushrooms, thinly
   sliced (1½ cups)
1 medium green pepper, cut into
   ½-inch strips
1 small onion, thinly sliced
¼ cup dry sherry

2 servings

In large plastic food-storage bag, combine flour, garlic powder and tarragon. Add duck strips. Shake to coat.

In 12-inch nonstick skillet, heat oil and margarine over medium heat. Add duck strips. Cook for 3 to 5 minutes, or until meat is browned, turning frequently. Add remaining ingredients, except sherry. Cook over medium heat for 3 to 5 minutes, or until vegetables are tender-crisp, stirring frequently. Add sherry. Cook for 5 to 8 minutes, or until meat is desired doneness. Serve over hot cooked wild rice, if desired.

Per Serving: Calories: 626 • Protein: 33 g.
• Carbohydrate: 28 g. • Fat: 39 g.
• Cholesterol: N/A • Sodium: 157 mg.
Exchanges: ¾ starch, 4 lean meat,
½ vegetable, 1 fruit, 5½ fat

Slow-cooker Duck & Dressing

Keith Sutton – Benton, Arkansas

½ cup margarine or butter
1 cup thinly sliced celery
1 cup chopped onions
7½ cups crumbled corn bread
5¾ cups duck broth or chicken
   broth
4 cups unseasoned dry bread
   crumbs
3½ cups cut-up cooked wild duck
   or goose (about 1 lb.)

2 cups crushed soda crackers
4 eggs, beaten
½ cup milk
2 teaspoons dried thyme or sage
   leaves
½ teaspoon baking powder
½ teaspoon freshly ground pepper

10 to 12 servings

In 10-inch nonstick skillet, melt margarine over medium heat. Add celery and onions. Cook for 2 to 3 minutes, or until vegetables are tender-crisp, stirring frequently.

In large mixing bowl, combine celery mixture and remaining ingredients. Spoon into 4-quart crockpot. Cover. Cook on High for 1 hour. Reduce heat to Low. Cook for 4 to 6 hours longer, or until liquid is absorbed.

Per Serving: Calories: 585 • Protein: 23 g. • Carbohydrate: 67 g. • Fat: 24 g.
• Cholesterol: 144 mg. • Sodium: 1590 mg.
Exchanges: 4½ starch, 1½ medium-fat meat, 3¼ fat

Soups, Stews & Chilies

Partridge & Pumpkin Soup

Bruno G. Mella, Executive Chef – New York, New York

2 cups whipping cream
2 tablespoons butter
1 clove garlic, minced
1 can (16 oz.) solid-pack pumpkin
1 cup chopped onions
2 tablespoons snipped fresh chives
1 sprig fresh thyme, finely chopped
2 cups cubed cantaloupe
   (¼-inch cubes)
2 cups peeled seeded cubed
   yellow summer squash
   (¼-inch cubes)
6 cups hot defatted chicken broth
12 oz. cooked partridge breast
   or substitute, cut into 2 ×
   ¼-inch strips

8 servings

Place cream in 2-quart heavy-bottomed saucepan. Cook over medium heat just until cream begins to simmer. Reduce heat to low. Simmer for 40 to 50 minutes, or until cream is reduced by half, stirring frequently with whisk. Remove from heat. Set aside.

Meanwhile, in 6-quart Dutch oven or stockpot, melt butter over medium-low heat. Add garlic. Cook for 2 minutes. Add pumpkin, onions and herbs. Cook over medium heat for 10 minutes, stirring frequently to prevent sticking. Stir in cantaloupe and squash. Blend in broth. Simmer for 25 to 30 minutes, or until flavors are blended.

In food processor or blender, process soup in several batches until smooth. Return processed soup to Dutch oven. Stir in partridge strips. Cook over medium heat for 4 to 6 minutes, or until hot. Top each serving with reduced cream and additional snipped fresh chives, if desired.

Per Serving: Calories: 374 • Protein: 19 g.
• Carbohydrate: 13 g. • Fat: 28 g.
• Cholesterol: N/A • Sodium: 818 mg.
Exchanges: 2 lean meat, 2 vegetable,
¼ fruit, 4½ fat

Dakota Pheasant Soup

Joyce Ingalls – Ingalls Prairie Wildfowl Hunts, Bryant, South Dakota

2 dressed pheasants or substitute
   (1½ to 2¼ lbs. each), cut up,
   skin on
9 cups water, divided
2 tablespoons snipped fresh parsley
1 teaspoon instant chicken
   bouillon granules
1 teaspoon salt
1 clove garlic, cut in half
½ teaspoon pepper

2½ cups thinly sliced celery
1 cup shredded carrots
½ cup chopped onion
¾ teaspoon dried thyme leaves
¼ to ½ teaspoon freshly
   ground pepper
1 bay leaf
3 cups uncooked dumpling
   noodles or extra-wide egg
   noodles

6 to 8 servings

In 6-quart Dutch oven or stockpot, combine pheasant pieces, 6 cups water, the parsley, boullion, salt, garlic and pepper. Bring to a boil over medium-high heat. Reduce heat to low. Simmer for 45 minutes to 1 hour, or until meat is tender. Remove from heat. Remove pheasant pieces from broth. Cool meat slightly. Strain broth and return to Dutch oven. Remove meat from bones. Discard bones and skin. Return meat to broth.

Add remaining 3 cups water and remaining ingredients, except noodles, to broth. Cook over medium heat for 5 to 8 minutes, or until vegetables are tender-crisp. Stir in noodles. Cook for 8 to 10 minutes, or until noodles are tender, stirring occasionally. Remove and discard bay leaf. Top each serving with seasoned croutons or crackers, if desired.

Per Serving: Calories: 288 • Protein: 41 g. • Carbohydrate: 14 g. • Fat: 7 g.
• Cholesterol: 161 mg. • Sodium: 496 mg.
Exchanges: ½ starch, 4½ lean meat, 1 vegetable

Wild Rice Pheasant Soup →

Irene M. Udovich – Udovich Guide Service,
Gheen, Minnesota

- 2 tablespoons margarine or
  butter
- ¼ cup finely chopped onion
- 1 clove garlic, minced
- ¼ cup all-purpose flour
- ½ teaspoon salt
- ½ teaspoon freshly ground
  pepper
- 4 cups chicken broth, divided
- 2½ cups cooked wild rice
- 2 cups cut-up cooked pheasant
  or substitute (about 10 oz.)
- 1 cup thinly sliced carrots
- 1 bay leaf
- 1 cup half-and-half
- 2 tablespoons dry sherry

8 servings

In 6-quart Dutch oven or stockpot,
melt margarine over medium heat.
Add onion and garlic. Cook for
2 to 3 minutes, or until onion is
tender, stirring frequently.

In 4-cup measure, combine flour,
salt and pepper. Blend in 2 cups
broth. Stir into onion mixture. Add
remaining 2 cups broth and remaining ingredients, except half-and-
half and sherry.

Bring to a boil over medium-high
heat. Reduce heat to low. Simmer
for 30 to 35 minutes, or until carrots are tender. Stir in half-and-half
and sherry. Simmer for 10 to 15
minutes longer, or until flavors are
blended. Remove and discard bay
leaf before serving.

Per Serving: Calories: 222 • Protein: 16 g.
• Carbohydrate: 18 g. • Fat: 9 g.
• Cholesterol: 54 mg. • Sodium: 700 mg.
Exchanges: 1 starch, 1½ lean meat,
½ vegetable, ¾ fat

Pheasant Soup & Dumplings

Gayle Grossman – Little Moran Hunting Club, Staples, Minnesota

- 2 dressed pheasants or substitute
  (1½ to 2¼ lbs. each), cut up,
  skin on
- 8 cups water, divided

DUMPLINGS:
- 1½ cups all-purpose flour
- 1 tablespoon snipped fresh parsley
- 2 teaspoons baking powder
- ½ teaspoon salt

- ⅔ cup buttermilk
- 1 egg, beaten
- 2 tablespoons butter, melted
- 2 cans (10¾ oz. each) condensed
  cream of chicken soup
- 1 pkg. (10 oz.) frozen mixed
  vegetables
- ½ teaspoon dried thyme leaves
- ½ teaspoon pepper

6 to 8 servings

In 6-quart Dutch oven or stockpot, combine pheasant pieces and 6 cups
water. Bring to a boil over medium-high heat. Reduce heat to low. Simmer
for 45 minutes to 1 hour, or until meat is tender. Remove from heat. Remove
pheasant pieces from broth. Cool meat slightly. Strain broth and return to
Dutch oven. Remove meat from bones. Discard bones and skin. Cut meat
into ¾-inch pieces. Return meat to broth.

In medium mixing bowl, combine flour, parsley, baking powder and salt. In
small mixing bowl, combine buttermilk, egg and butter. Add milk mixture
to flour mixture. Stir just until dry ingredients are moistened. Set dumpling batter aside.

Add remaining 2 cups water to broth. Bring to a boil over medium-high
heat. Stir in condensed soup, vegetables, thyme and pepper. Return soup to
a boil. Drop batter by rounded tablespoons into hot soup. Reduce heat to
low. Cover. Cook for 15 to 20 minutes, or until dumplings are light and
springy to the touch and no longer doughy. Garnish each serving with
additional snipped fresh parsley, if desired.

Per Serving: Calories: 438 • Protein: 45 g. • Carbohydrate: 30 g. • Fat: 14 g.
• Cholesterol: 188 mg. • Sodium: 994 mg.
Exchanges: 2 starch, 5 lean meat

K.B.'s Duck & Sausage Gumbo

Keith Sutton – Benton, Arkansas

¼ cup plus 2 tablespoons
    vegetable oil*
½ cup all-purpose flour
1 cup chopped onions
1 cup chopped green pepper
1 cup chopped red pepper
1 cup sliced celery
5 cups water, divided
1½ cups cut-up cooked wild duck
    (about 8 oz.)
1 lb. smoked sausage links, sliced
½ cup sliced green onions
1 clove garlic, minced
1 teaspoon salt
1 teaspoon pepper
½ teaspoon dried thyme leaves
2¼ cups sliced fresh or frozen
    okra (½-inch slices)
1 teaspoon Worcestershire sauce
½ to 1 teaspoon red pepper sauce
1 teaspoon filé powder

10 to 12 servings

In 6-quart Dutch oven or stockpot, heat oil over medium-low heat. Gradually add flour, stirring constantly with whisk. Cook over medium heat for 25 to 35 minutes, or until mixture is dark golden brown, stirring occasionally. (Do not burn.)

Add chopped onions, chopped peppers and celery. Cook over medium-high heat for 2 to 3 minutes, or until vegetables are tender-crisp, stirring frequently. Add 3 cups water, the duck pieces, sausage, green onions, garlic, salt, pepper and thyme. Bring to a boil. Reduce heat to low. Simmer, covered, for 1 hour.

Add remaining 2 cups water, the okra, Worcestershire sauce and red pepper sauce. Simmer, uncovered, over low heat for 1 hour. Remove from heat. Stir in filé powder. Serve over hot cooked rice, if desired.

*Two tablespoons bacon drippings may be substituted for 2 tablespoons vegetable oil, if desired.

Note: Additional cooking makes filé powder tough and stringy. Add filé powder only to portion of gumbo you plan to consume immediately. Add remaining filé powder to reheated leftover portion.

Per Serving: Calories: 293 • Protein: 15 g. • Carbohydrate: 11 g. • Fat: 21 g.
• Cholesterol: 43 mg. • Sodium: 789 mg.
Exchanges: ¼ starch, 1½ medium-fat meat, 1¼ vegetable, 2¾ fat

Grandpa's Favorite Rabbit Stew →

Keith Sutton – Benton, Arkansas

⅓ cup all-purpose flour
2 teaspoons salt, divided
1 teaspoon freshly ground pepper, divided
2 dressed wild rabbits or substitute (1½ to 2 lbs. each), cut up
3 slices bacon
3 tablespoons vegetable oil
3 cups water
4 cups cubed red potatoes (4 medium), ½-inch cubes
1½ cups chopped carrots
2 medium onions, sliced
2 cloves garlic, minced
1 cup sour cream
¼ cup snipped fresh parsley
2 to 3 teaspoons paprika

8 to 10 servings

In large plastic food-storage bag, combine flour, 1 teaspoon salt and ½ teaspoon pepper. Add rabbit pieces. Shake to coat. Set aside. In 6-quart Dutch oven or stockpot, cook bacon over medium heat for 5 to 7 minutes, or until brown and crisp, turning occasionally. Drain on paper-towel-lined plate. Cool slightly. Crumble bacon. Set aside.

In same Dutch oven, heat bacon drippings and oil over medium heat. Add rabbit pieces. Cook for 8 to 10 minutes, or until meat is browned, turning occasionally. Drain and discard oil from Dutch oven.

To same Dutch oven, add remaining 1 teaspoon salt, ½ teaspoon pepper, the bacon, water, potatoes, carrots, onions and garlic. Bring to a boil over medium-high heat. Reduce heat to low. Cover. Simmer for 45 minutes to 1 hour, or until meat is tender. Remove from heat. Stir in sour cream, parsley and paprika. Serve immediately.

Per Serving: Calories: 362 • Protein: 31 g. • Carbohydrate: 22 g. • Fat: 16 g. • Cholesterol: 118 mg. • Sodium: 576 mg. Exchanges: ¾ starch, 3½ lean meat, 2¼ vegetable, 1 fat

Wild Game Jambalaya

Barbara Canton and Brian DeCicco – Affairs to Remember Catering, Pawling, New York

¼ cup olive oil
1½ cups chopped red peppers
1 cup chopped onions
1 cup chopped green pepper
1 cup thinly sliced celery
½ cup sliced green onions
2 medium jalapeño peppers, chopped
2 cloves garlic, minced
1 lb. boneless skinless pheasant breast or substitute, cut into ½-inch cubes
1 lb. boneless skinless wild duck breast or substitute, cut into ½-inch cubes
8 oz. smoked pheasant or turkey sausage links, cut into ½-inch pieces
8 oz. bulk sweet Italian sausage, crumbled
8 oz. boneless venison loin steak or substitute, cut into 1-inch cubes
8 oz. fresh medium shrimp, shelled and deveined, each cut in half lengthwise (optional)
1 can (28 oz.) Roma tomatoes, undrained and cut up
2 cups cooked Basmati rice
2 teaspoons cayenne
1 teaspoon dried thyme leaves
½ teaspoon pepper
½ teaspoon salt

14 to 16 servings

In 6-quart Dutch oven or stockpot, heat oil over medium heat. Add vegetables, pheasant cubes, duck cubes, sausages and venison cubes. Cook for 10 to 12 minutes, or until meat is browned and vegetables are tender-crisp, stirring occasionally.

Add shrimp. Cook over medium heat for 3 to 5 minutes, or until shrimp are firm and opaque, stirring frequently. Add remaining ingredients. Bring to a boil. Reduce heat to low. Simmer for 30 to 35 minutes, or until flavors are blended.

Per Serving: Calories: 246 • Protein: 22 g • Carbohydrate: 13 g. • Fat: 12 g. • Cholesterol: N/A • Sodium: 420 mg. Exchanges: ½ starch, 2½ medium-fat meat, 1 vegetable

Crockpot Coon Stew

Thomas K. Squier – Aberdeen, North Carolina

3 to 4 lbs. well-trimmed raccoon pieces
8 cups water
3 cups chopped onions
2 cups sliced carrots
2 cups cubed red potatoes (4 small), 1-inch cubes
2 cups beef broth
1 can (15 oz.) tomato sauce
4 oz. fresh mushrooms, chopped (1½ cups)
1 cup sliced fresh or frozen okra
1 cup sliced yellow summer squash or zucchini squash
1 cup shredded green cabbage
1 cup chopped celery
¼ cup dry red wine
1 tablespoon Italian seasoning
4 bay leaves
¼ teaspoon pepper

In 6-quart Dutch oven or stockpot, combine raccoon pieces and water. Bring to a boil over high heat. Reduce heat to low. Cover. Simmer for 1½ to 2 hours, or until meat is tender. Drain and discard broth. Cool meat slightly. Remove meat from bones. Discard bones. Cut meat into ¾-inch pieces.

In 4-quart crockpot, combine meat and remaining ingredients. Cover. Cook on High for 1 hour. Reduce heat to Low. Cook for 8 hours, or until vegetables are tender and flavors are blended. Remove and discard bay leaves before serving.

Per Serving: Calories: 355 • Protein: 28 g. • Carbohydrate: 35 g. • Fat: 12 g. • Cholesterol: N/A • Sodium: N/A
Exchanges: ¾ starch, 2½ lean meat, 4¾ vegetable, 1 fat

6 servings

Indiana Rabbit Stew

Ray Harper – Evansville, Indiana

½ cup all-purpose flour
½ teaspoon salt
¼ teaspoon pepper
2 dressed wild rabbits or substitute
    (1½ to 2 lbs. each), cut up
3 tablespoons bacon drippings or
    vegetable oil
4 cups chicken broth
1 cup thinly sliced celery
1 cup chopped onions
5 cups cubed red potatoes
    (5 medium), ¾-inch cubes
2 cans (15 oz. each) tomato sauce
8 oz. fresh mushrooms, sliced
    (3 cups)
2½ cups thinly sliced carrots
1 large green pepper, cut into
    ½-inch chunks

10 to 12 servings

In large plastic food-storage bag, combine flour, salt and pepper. Add rabbit pieces. Shake to coat. In 6-quart Dutch oven or stockpot, heat drippings over medium heat. Add rabbit pieces. Cook for 8 to 10 minutes, or until meat is browned, turning occasionally. Add broth, celery and onions. Reduce heat to low. Cover. Simmer for 45 minutes to 1 hour, or until meat is tender, stirring occasionally.

Remove from heat. Remove rabbit pieces from broth. Cool meat slightly. Remove meat from bones. Discard bones. Cut meat into ¾-inch pieces. Return meat to broth. Add remaining ingredients. Bring to a boil over medium heat. Reduce heat to medium-low. Cover. Simmer for 20 to 25 minutes, or until stew thickens slightly and vegetables are tender, stirring occasionally.

Per Serving: Calories: 267 • Protein: 28 g.
• Carbohydrate: 26 g. • Fat: 6 g.
• Cholesterol: 88 mg. • Sodium: 941 mg.
Exchanges: 1 starch, 2¾ lean meat,
2 vegetable

Hunting Camp Stew ↑

William P. Whitney – Big Flats, New York

¼ cup all-purpose flour
2 tablespoons plus 1 teaspoon
    chili powder, divided
2 tablespoons paprika
2 lbs. venison stew meat or
    substitute (well trimmed),
    cut into 1-inch cubes
3 tablespoons olive oil
1 cup chopped onions
1 clove garlic, minced
2 cans (14½ oz. each) stewed
    tomatoes, undrained
2 cups water
2 teaspoons ground cinnamon
1 teaspoon instant beef bouillon
    granules
½ teaspoon ground cloves
½ teaspoon crushed red pepper
    flakes (optional)
2 cups peeled cubed red potatoes
    (2 medium), ½-inch cubes
2 cups chopped carrots

4 to 6 servings

In large plastic food-storage bag, combine flour, 1 teaspoon chili powder and the paprika. Add venison cubes. Shake to coat. In 6-quart Dutch oven or stockpot, heat oil over medium-high heat. Add venison cubes, onions and garlic. Cook for 15 to 18 minutes, or until meat is browned, stirring occasionally.

Stir in remaining 2 tablespoons chili powder and remaining ingredients, except potatoes and carrots. Bring to a boil. Reduce heat to low. Cover. Simmer for 1½ to 2 hours, or until meat is tender, stirring occasionally. Stir in potatoes and carrots. Simmer, uncovered, for 30 to 45 minutes, or until vegetables are tender, stirring occasionally.

Per Serving: Calories: 386 • Protein: 39 g. • Carbohydrate: 33 g. • Fat: 12 g.
• Cholesterol: 129 mg. • Sodium: 650 mg.
Exchanges: 1 starch, 4 lean meat, 3½ vegetable

Creole Okra with Venison Meatballs

"This dish freezes well. It is especially delicious served over rice with crowder peas, cucumber salad and corn bread."
John and Denise Phillips – Fairfield, Alabama

2 lbs. lean ground venison or substitute, crumbled
2 eggs
½ cup unseasoned dry bread crumbs
½ teaspoon salt
¼ teaspoon pepper
2 tablespoons vegetable oil
1½ cups chopped onions
1 cup chopped green pepper
1 cup thinly sliced celery
2 cloves garlic, minced
½ teaspoon dried thyme leaves
½ teaspoon dried basil leaves
4½ cups sliced fresh or frozen okra (½-inch slices)
2 cans (14½ oz. each) whole tomatoes, undrained
½ cup water
½ to 1 teaspoon cayenne

8 to 10 servings

In medium mixing bowl, combine ground venison, eggs, bread crumbs, salt and pepper. Shape mixture into 40 meatballs, 1½ inches in diameter. In 6-quart Dutch oven or stockpot, heat oil over medium heat. Add half of meatballs. Cook for 5 to 7 minutes, or until meatballs are browned, turning occasionally. Using slotted spoon, remove meatballs from Dutch oven. Cover to keep warm. Repeat with remaining meatballs. Set aside.

To same Dutch oven, add onions, green pepper, celery, garlic, thyme and basil. Cook over medium heat for 2 to 3 minutes, or until vegetables are tender-crisp, stirring frequently.

Add meatballs and remaining ingredients to vegetable mixture. Cook over medium-low heat for 30 to 35 minutes, or until mixture is hot and flavors are blended, stirring occasionally. Serve over hot cooked rice, if desired.

Per Serving: Calories: 346 • Protein: 21 g. • Carbohydrate: 14 g. • Fat: 22 g. • Cholesterol: 124 mg. • Sodium: 356 mg.
Exchanges: ¼ starch, 2½ lean meat, 2 vegetable, 3 fat

Wood-stove Stew →

Col. Lyle B. Otto – Gig Harbor, Washington

¼ cup all-purpose flour
½ teaspoon salt
¼ teaspoon pepper
1½ lbs. moose stew meat or
    substitute (well trimmed),
    cut into 1-inch cubes
3 slices bacon, chopped
1 clove garlic, minced
4 cups water
½ cup dry red wine
2 tablespoons Worcestershire
    sauce
1 tablespoon lemon juice
1 teaspoon instant beef bouillon
    granules
½ teaspoon dried thyme leaves
3 cups whole baby carrots
4 small onions, sliced
2 cups quartered red potatoes
    (4 small)
½ cup sliced celery
1 cup frozen peas

6 to 8 servings

In large plastic food-storage bag, combine flour, salt and pepper. Add moose cubes. Shake to coat. Set aside. In 6-quart Dutch oven or stockpot, cook bacon over medium heat until brown and crisp, stirring occasionally. Add moose cubes and garlic. Cook over medium heat for 5 to 7 minutes, or until meat is browned, stirring occasionally.

Stir in water, wine, Worcestershire sauce, juice, bouillon and thyme. Bring to a boil. Reduce heat to low. Cover. Simmer for 1 to 1½ hours, or until meat is almost tender, stirring occasionally.

Add carrots, onions, potatoes and celery. Re-cover. Simmer for 45 to 50 minutes, or until meat and vegetables are tender. Add peas. Re-cover. Simmer for 5 to 10 minutes, or until peas are hot.

Per Serving: Calories: 256 • Protein: 23 g. • Carbohydrate: 26 g. • Fat: 26 g. • Cholesterol: 56 mg. • Sodium: 445 mg. Exchanges: 1 starch, 2¼ lean meat, 2 vegetable

Venison Stew

Wayne Chamberlain – Pequot Lakes, Minnesota

½ cup all-purpose flour
2 teaspoons Mrs. Dash® all-natural
    seasoning, divided
¼ teaspoon pepper
2 lbs. venison stew meat or
    substitute (well trimmed), cut
    into 1-inch cubes
3 tablespoons vegetable oil
3 cups water
3 cups sliced red potatoes
    (4 medium), ¼-inch slices
2 cups thinly sliced carrots

2 cups coarsely chopped green
    cabbage
2 cups beef broth
1 can (15½ oz.) corn, drained
1 can (14½ oz.) diced tomatoes,
    undrained
1 cup catsup
½ cup chopped onion
¼ cup barbecue sauce
½ teaspoon dried dill weed
    (optional)

6 to 8 servings

In large plastic food-storage bag, combine flour, 1 teaspoon all-natural seasoning and the pepper. Add venison cubes. Shake to coat. In 6-quart Dutch oven or stockpot, heat oil over medium-high heat. Add venison cubes. Cook for 6 to 8 minutes, or until meat is browned, stirring occasionally.

Stir in remaining 1 teaspoon all-natural seasoning and remaining ingredients. Bring to a boil. Reduce heat to low. Cover. Simmer for 1 to 1½ hours, or until meat and vegetables are tender, stirring occasionally.

Per Serving: Calories: 375 • Protein: 32 g. • Carbohydrate: 44 g. • Fat: 9 g. • Cholesterol: 96 mg. • Sodium: 941 mg. Exchanges: 1¾ starch, 2¾ lean meat, 3½ vegetable, ¼ fat

Venison Stew & Dumplings

Jay "D" Flattum – Lofton Ridge Deer Farm, Chisago City, Minnesota

¼ cup all-purpose flour
1½ teaspoons salt
½ teaspoon freshly ground pepper
2 lbs. venison stew meat or substitute (well trimmed),
    cut into 1-inch cubes
3 tablespoons vegetable oil
5 cups water
2 teaspoons sugar
1 teaspoon Worcestershire sauce
1 clove garlic, minced
1 bay leaf
6 small red potatoes, cut into halves
6 medium carrots, diagonally sliced (½-inch slices)
6 small onions, cut into quarters
2 stalks celery, diagonally sliced (1-inch lengths)
1 cup buttermilk baking mix
1 tablespoon snipped fresh parsley
1 egg, beaten
3 tablespoons milk

6 to 8 servings

In large plastic food-storage bag, combine flour, salt and pepper. Add venison cubes. Shake to coat. In 6-quart Dutch oven or stockpot, heat oil over medium heat. Add venison cubes. Cook for 8 to 10 minutes, or until meat is browned, stirring occasionally. Add water, sugar, Worcestershire sauce, garlic and bay leaf. Bring to a boil over medium-high heat. Reduce heat to low. Cover. Simmer for 1¼ to 1½ hours, or until meat is tender, stirring occasionally. Add potatoes, carrots, onions and celery. Cook, un-covered, over medium heat for 15 minutes.

In medium mixing bowl, combine baking mix and parsley. Add egg and milk. Stir just until dry in-gredients are moistened. Drop batter by heaping tablespoons into stew. Cook for 10 minutes. Cover. Cook for 10 to 15 minutes longer, or until dumplings are light and springy to the touch and no longer doughy. Remove and discard bay leaf before serving.

Per Serving: Calories: 398 • Protein: 32 g. • Carbohydrate: 42 g. • Fat: 11 g. • Cholesterol: 124 mg. • Sodium: 699 mg.
Exchanges: 2 starch, 2¾ lean meat, 2½ vegetable, ½ fat

Lyle's Venison Chili with Texas-style Corn Bread

Col. Lyle B. Otto – Gig Harbor, Washington

CHILI:

- 2 tablespoons vegetable oil
- 2½ lbs. lean ground venison or substitute, crumbled
- 1¾ cups chopped onions
- 2 cloves garlic, minced
- 1 can (28 oz.) whole tomatoes, cut up, undrained
- 1 can (8 oz.) tomato sauce
- 1 can (4 oz.) chopped green chilies, drained
- 4 jalapeño peppers, seeded and chopped
- 2 tablespoons chili powder
- 1 teaspoon salt
- 1 teaspoon pepper
- 1 teaspoon Worcestershire sauce
- 2 cans (15½ oz. each) dark red kidney beans, undrained
- 1¼ cups chopped green peppers

CORN BREAD:

- 1 cup yellow cornmeal
- 1 cup all-purpose flour
- 3 tablespoons sugar
- 2 teaspoons baking powder
- ¾ teaspoon salt
- ½ cup canned Mexican-style corn, drained
- 1 cup buttermilk
- ¼ cup canned chopped green chilies, drained
- 1 egg, beaten
- 3 tablespoons vegetable oil

8 to 10 servings

In 6-quart Dutch oven or stockpot, heat 2 tablespoons oil over medium heat. Add ground venison, onions and garlic. Cook for 10 to 15 minutes, or until meat is no longer pink and vegetables are tender, stirring frequently. Add remaining chili ingredients, except beans and green peppers. Mix well. Bring to a boil. Reduce heat to low. Cover. Simmer for 1 hour, stirring occasionally. Add beans and green peppers. Re-cover. Simmer for 15 to 20 minutes, or until green peppers are tender, stirring occasionally.

Meanwhile, heat oven to 400°F. Heavily grease 10-inch cast-iron or ovenproof skillet with shortening. Set aside.

In medium mixing bowl, combine cornmeal, flour, sugar, baking powder and salt. Stir in corn. In small mixing bowl, combine buttermilk, chilies, egg and oil. Add buttermilk mixture to cornmeal mixture. Stir just until dry ingredients are moistened. Spread batter in prepared skillet. Bake for 20 to 25 minutes, or until wooden pick inserted in center comes out clean. Serve chili with wedges of corn bread.

Per Serving: Calories: 614 • Protein: 32 g. • Carbohydrate: 52 g. • Fat: 31 g. • Cholesterol: 124 mg. • Sodium: 1286 mg.
Exchanges: 2¾ starch, 2¾ medium-fat meat, 2 vegetable, 3½ fat

Wild Bob's Wild Elk Chili

Bob Lee Innes – Maple Plain, Minnesota

2 lbs. lean ground elk or substitute, crumbled
2 cups thinly sliced celery
1 cup chopped onions
2 cloves garlic, minced
3 cans (10¾ oz. each) condensed cream of tomato soup

2 cans (15½ oz. each) dark red kidney beans, undrained
1 can (29 oz.) tomato purée
1 can (6 oz.) tomato paste
2 tablespoons chili powder
1 teaspoon seasoned salt

10 to 12 servings

In 6-quart Dutch oven or stockpot, combine ground elk, celery, onions and garlic. Cook over medium heat for 10 to 15 minutes, or until meat is browned, stirring occasionally. Drain. Stir in remaining ingredients. Bring to a boil over medium-high heat. Reduce heat to low. Cover. Simmer for 45 minutes to 1 hour, or until flavors are blended, stirring occasionally. Sprinkle each serving with shredded Cheddar cheese and sliced green onion, if desired.

Per Serving: Calories: 357 • Protein: 21 g. • Carbohydrate: 33 g. • Fat: 17 g.
• Cholesterol: 49 mg. • Sodium: 1227 mg.
Exchanges: 1½ starch, 1¾ lean meat, 1¾ vegetable, 2½ fat

← Mike Hanlon's Chunky-style Venison Chili

"Mike, an ex-marine, goes with me to faraway deer camps. His rabbit in wine is a camp special, but he can also cook up a mean pot of chili."
    Mike Roberts – South Meriden, Connecticut

1 tablespoon vegetable oil
½ lb. lean ground venison or substitute, crumbled
1 lb. venison stew meat or substitute (well trimmed), cut into ¾-inch cubes
2 cans (16 oz. each) dark red kidney beans, undrained
1 can (28 oz.) whole tomatoes, undrained and cut up
1½ cups chopped green peppers
1 cup chopped onions
1 can (6 oz.) tomato paste
5 cloves garlic, minced
1 tablespoon chili powder
1 teaspoon sugar
½ teaspoon pepper
½ teaspoon salt

6 to 8 servings

In 6-quart Dutch oven or stockpot, heat oil over medium-high heat. Add ground venison and venison cubes. Cook for 8 to 10 minutes, or until meat is no longer pink, stirring occasionally. Drain.

Stir in remaining ingredients. Bring to a boil. Reduce heat to low. Simmer, partially covered, for 4 to 5 hours, or until meat is very tender, stirring occasionally. Garnish each serving with sour cream, shredded cheese and sliced green onions, if desired.

Per Serving: Calories: 307 • Protein: 27 g.
• Carbohydrate: 30 g. • Fat: 10 g.
• Cholesterol: 74 mg. • Sodium: 911 mg.
Exchanges: 1¼ starch, 2½ lean meat, 2 vegetable, ½ fat

Wawa's Chili ↑

Warren C. Ewald, Sr. – Levittown, New York

- 2 tablespoons vegetable oil
- 2 lbs. elk stew meat or substitute (well trimmed), cut into ½-inch cubes
- 2 cups chopped onions
- 2 cans (14½ oz. each) diced tomatoes, undrained
- 1 cup water
- 1 cup chili sauce
- 4 pickled pepperoncini peppers, stems removed, chopped
- 1 teaspoon chili powder
- 2 bay leaves
- ¼ teaspoon pepper
- 2 cans (15½ oz. each) dark red kidney beans, rinsed and drained
- 2 cups coarsely chopped green peppers

6 to 8 servings

In 6-quart Dutch oven or stockpot, heat oil over medium heat. Add elk cubes and onions. Cook for 6 to 8 minutes, or until meat is no longer pink, stirring occasionally. Drain. Stir in remaining ingredients, except beans and green peppers. Bring to a boil over medium-high heat. Reduce heat to low. Cover. Simmer for 45 minutes to 1 hour, or until meat is tender, stirring occasionally. Stir in beans and peppers. Re-cover. Simmer for 15 to 20 minutes, or until green peppers are tender, stirring occasionally.

Per Serving: Calories: 297 • Protein: 34 g. • Carbohydrate: 27 g. • Fat: 6 g. • Cholesterol: 62 mg. • Sodium: 938 mg.
Exchanges: 1 starch, 3¼ lean meat, 2 vegetable

White Bean & Pheasant Chili ↑

The Hunting and Fishing Library®

- 2 tablespoons margarine or butter
- 1 cup sliced green onions
- 3 tablespoons all-purpose flour
- 2 cups chicken broth
- 3½ cups cut-up cooked pheasant or substitute (about 1 lb.)
- 1 can (15 oz.) Great Northern beans, rinsed and drained
- 1 can (11 oz.) corn with red and green peppers, drained
- ¾ cup half-and-half
- 1 can (4 oz.) chopped green chilies, undrained
- 1¾ teaspoons ground cumin
- 2 tablespoons fresh lime juice

6 servings

In 3-quart saucepan, melt margarine over medium heat. Add onions. Cook for 2 to 3 minutes, or until onions are tender-crisp, stirring frequently. Stir in flour, 1 tablespoon at a time, stirring well after each addition. Blend in broth, stirring constantly. Add remaining ingredients, except juice. Bring to a boil, stirring frequently. Reduce heat to low. Cover. Simmer for 10 to 15 minutes, or until chili is slightly thickened and flavors are blended, stirring occasionally. Stir in juice. Garnish each serving with grated lime peel and serve with tortilla chips, if desired.

Per Serving: Calories: 314 • Protein: 29 g. • Carbohydrate: 24 g. • Fat: 12 g. • Cholesterol: 97 mg. • Sodium: 835 mg.
Exchanges: 1⅓ starch, 3½ lean meat, ½ vegetable

Game Sausages & Smokehouse Specialties

There are few things more satisfying than serving plump, tasty sausages you've made yourself, or a deliciously scented hickory-smoked game roast.

The traditional arts of sausage making and smoking are enjoying a renaissance. With good mail-order sources, special sausage-making equipment and ingredients are available to anyone. When you make it yourself, you'll have the satisfaction of knowing exactly what went into your sausage.

Smoking, too, is within the reach of almost any cook with a little ambition. Whether you use a standard covered grill to smoke, convert an old refrigerator into a smoker or buy a deluxe insulated smokehouse, you'll be able to turn out smoked delicacies that couldn't be bought for any price. Smoking your own homemade sausages is the ultimate combination of these old-time arts.

Temperature control when smoking is extremely important for proper drying of sausages and for quality control. Most fresh sausages are cooked by methods other than smoking. They may be smoked at low temperatures for flavoring, but are later grilled, broiled or panfried. Salami and other cured sausages, however, receive no further cooking.

Because low smokehouse temperatures and airtight casings create an ideal environment for bacteria growth, we recommend adding *cure* (page 113) to all sausage that is smoked, to prevent the growth of organisms that cause food poisoning. Roasts, birds and other whole pieces of meat that are *smoke-cooked* don't need cure, since they're cooked quickly, with higher temperatures, and smoke is used only for flavor.

On the following pages, we explain how to make several fresh game sausages and include detailed step-by-step sequences for using natural and synthetic casings. We'll take you through the steps necessary to make your own cured, smoked salami and jerky. Start with the basics, and you'll have great success making your own smoked specialties.

Game Sausages

For big game sausages, use trimmed meat from any part of the animal; the meat doesn't need to be tender. Game bird sausages work well with any combination of breast or thigh meat. Generally, fatty pork butt or plain pork fat is added to the lean meat. Be sure to specify hard pork *back fat* when you order the fat from your butcher; tell the butcher what you'll be using it for to be sure you get the right thing. (Back fat is not the same as *fatback,* which is fat that has been salted and dried). Lard is too soft and will produce a greasy sausage. It should not be used.

Keep meat-grinder blades sharp when grinding meat for sausage. Dull blades squeeze juices from the meat, resulting in dry, less-flavorful sausage.

If your grinder slows down during use or if the texture of the meat suddenly becomes fine and mushy, partially disassemble the grinder and check the blades and plate. Sinew and other tough material can get caught in the mechanism, causing poor performance. Clean the blade and plate, then continue. You may need some help when making sausages. One person can turn the crank, while the other guides the casings off the horn and twists the links.

Venison and other hoofed big game can take the place of lean beef in any sausage recipe. Bear or boar can be susbtituted for lean pork in other recipes, but you'll still need to add pork fat.

SAUSAGE-MAKING SUPPLIES & EQUIPMENT include (1) optional heavy-duty sausage stuffer, helpful for large quantities; (2) large nonmetallic mixing bowl or tub; (3) kitchen scale; (4) kitchen twine; (5) sausage casings; (6) meat grinder with 2 grinding plates and stuffing horns; and specialty ingredients and optional equipment for cured sausages, including (7) powdered dextrose, (8) soy protein concentrate, (9) premixed cure/seasoning blends, (10) curing powder or curing salt, and (11) sausage pricker for eliminating air bubbles.

WASH all equipment thoroughly in very hot, soapy water prior to making sausages. Rinse and refrigerate equipment until cool before using. Wash hands and scrub fingernails with nail brush. Scrub countertops and cutting boards with soapy water, and rinse well.

KEEP meat as cold as possible during sausage making. If meat is to be ground twice, chill it thoroughly and wash and refrigerate grinder between grindings. When working with a large batch of meat, grind only a small portion at a time and leave the rest refrigerated.

GRIND lean meat separately from fat for juicier fresh sausages. Cut fat into chunks, partially freeze it, then grind it finer than the meat. Mix ground meat and ground fat together. This way, the fat will be more evenly distributed and there won't be any large pieces in your sausage.

USE a cure for all sausages that will be smoked, to prevent botulism, a type of food poisoning. For a fresh-sausage recipe that makes 5 pounds, *substitute* 8 level teaspoons Morton® TenderQuick® mix for 5½ level teaspoons canning/pickling salt; or, *add* 1 level teaspoon Prague Powder No. 1 to the salt already in recipe.

SPRINKLE mixed dry seasonings over *coarsely* ground meat. Mix well, and refrigerate overnight to blend flavors. Mix with liquid called for in recipe, then grind through finer plate and stuff immediately. If using already-ground meat, mix dry seasonings with liquid before adding to meat.

CHOOSE (1) lamb casings for breakfast sausages; (2) collagen casings for snack sticks; (3) hog casings for Polish-size sausages; or (4) synthetic-fibrous casings for salami. Fresh-sausage recipes need not be cased; form into (5) patties, and fry or broil.

113

Using Synthetic & Natural Casings

Synthetic casings used in this book include edible 19 mm collagen casings used for snack sticks and 3½-inch synthetic-fibrous casings used for salami, which are peeled and discarded before the sausage is eaten. Salami-size casings can also be made from clean muslin. Before stuffing, sew one end shut in a half-circle and turn right side out to prevent unraveling. Stuff tightly and tie off as directed below.

Natural sausage casings include lamb casings (22 to 24 mm), which are used for breakfast links, and hog casings (32 to 35 mm is a common size), which are used for Italian, Polish and country-style links. A butcher shop that specializes in sausages may sell you a hank, a bundle of casings packed in salt. You can also order casings from specialty sources (see page 128).

The casing you select is usually based on the sausage you'll be making. Natural casings are usually used for fresh sausages, since they are tender and edible. Snack sticks use collagen casings, which are smaller than the smallest natural casings. Synthetic-fibrous casings are perfect for salami, and are easier to find than natural alternatives.

Preparing & Stuffing Synthetic Casings

SOAK synthetic-fibrous casings in a mixture of 3 tablespoons white vinegar to 2 quarts lukewarm water for 30 minutes, or as directed by manufacturer. The vinegar helps the casing to peel smoothly from the finished salami and helps prevent mold growth. Wet a home-made muslin casing before stuffing.

WRAP the middle of a 20-inch piece of kitchen string tightly around one end of the casing several times; then fan out the end like butterfly wings. Wrap one end of the string tightly around one wing several times. Repeat on the other side. Wrap both ends of string around main neck again. Tie securely.

STUFF with sausage mixture by hand or with a stuffing horn. Pack casing tightly, squeezing to force out air pockets. Tie off with butterfly knot; make loop in string for hanging sausage. If there are small air bubbles trapped under the surface, pierce casing with sterilized pin or with sausage pricker.

114

SPREAD OUT a hank of salted casings carefully on clean work surface. Find the beginning of the hank, and gently pull one length out of the bundle until it is free, being careful not to twist the remainder of the lengths. Remove as many lengths as you need. Resalt and freeze the remainder for future use.

OPEN one end of the casing, and slip the end over a faucet. Hold your hand over the casing to keep it from slipping off. Run a steady, medium stream of cold water through the casing until it is completely filled and the water runs through. Continue flushing for a few minutes. Rinse the outside of the casing.

PLACE the rinsed casing in a large measuring cup filled with cold water after draining out all water and air from the casing. Let one end of the casing hang over the edge of the cup. Rinse remaining casings, adding them to the measuring cup, until you've rinsed all the casings you will need.

SLIP one end of a rinsed, wet casing over the sausage-stuffing horn; push until the end of the casing is at the back end of the horn. Continue pushing until the entire length is gathered onto the horn. Pull the casing forward until about 1 inch hangs over the open end of the horn.

TURN the crank of the sausage stuffer slowly until some of the sausage mixture comes out of the horn. Tie off the end of the casing with kitchen string, pinching off a small bit of meat. The pinching helps eliminate air at the end of the link. Continue cranking until sausage is desired length; have a helper guide the link away from the horn.

TWIST the first link several times; then crank until a second link is formed. Support both links with one hand while using the other to keep the casing on the horn until it is firmly filled. Be sure to let the casing slip off easily before it overfills and breaks. Continue twisting and filling; keep casings on horn wet so they slip off without sticking.

Game Bird Sausage

"These suit Sunday breakfasts or a light lunch."
Annette Bignami – Moscow, Indiana

¾ lb. lean ground veal or pork, crumbled
½ lb. boneless skinless pheasant breast and thigh
  or substitute, cut into 1-inch pieces
½ lb. pork back fat, cut into 1-inch pieces
1 cup finely chopped onions
½ cup unseasoned dry bread crumbs
2 eggs
⅓ cup milk
1 teaspoon canning/pickling salt
1 teaspoon white pepper
1 teaspoon ground nutmeg
½ teaspoon chili powder
  Natural sheep casings (22 to 24 mm)

14 sausages (about 2 oz. each)

In large mixing bowl, combine meats and back fat. In medium mixing bowl, combine remaining ingredients, except casings. Add to meat mixture. Mix by hand until ingredients are evenly distributed. Grind mixture through a 3/16-inch plate. Cover with plastic wrap. Refrigerate until ready to stuff. Prepare and stuff casings as directed (page 115), using a ½-inch horn and twisting off in 4-inch links. Sausages may be panfried or grilled. Wrap tightly and freeze any remaining sausages for future use.

Variation: Game Bird Sausage Patties: Prepare recipe as directed above, except omit casings. Shape meat mixture evenly into patties. Layer patties with wax paper. Stack patties, wrap in foil and freeze no longer than 2 months.

Per Serving: Calories: 238 • Protein: 10 g. • Carbohydrate: 4 g. • Fat: 20 g. • Cholesterol: 81 mg. • Sodium: 229 mg. Exchanges: ¼ starch, 1 lean meat, ¼ vegetable, 3¼ fat

Italian-style Sausage

William P. Whitney – Big Flats, New York

5 lbs. lean ground venison or substitute, crumbled
5 lbs. ground pork, crumbled
5 teaspoons fennel seed
5 teaspoons crushed red pepper flakes
5 teaspoons chili powder
5 teaspoons dried oregano leaves
2½ teaspoons canning/pickling salt
1½ teaspoons garlic powder
1¼ teaspoons freshly ground pepper
  Natural hog casings (29 to 32 mm)

32 sausages (about 5 oz. each)

In large mixing bowl, combine ground venison and ground pork. In small mixing bowl, combine remaining ingredients, except casings. Sprinkle seasoning mixture evenly over meat. Mix by hand until ingredients are evenly distributed. Cover with plastic wrap. Refrigerate until ready to stuff.

Prepare and stuff casings as directed (page 115), using a ¾-inch horn and twisting off in 6-inch links. Sausages may be panfried with sliced onion and green pepper, if desired, or grilled. Wrap tightly and freeze any remaining sausages for future use.

Variation: Italian-style Sausage Patties: Prepare recipe as directed above, except omit casings. Shape meat mixture evenly into patties. Layer patties with wax paper. Stack patties, wrap in foil and freeze no longer than 2 months.

Per Serving: Calories: 376 • Protein: 25 g. • Carbohydrate: 1 g. • Fat: 29 g. • Cholesterol: 114 mg. • Sodium: 189 mg. Exchanges: 3¾ high-fat meat

Venison Sausage Patties

"This is my wife's recipe. It's the only one we use for sausage."
Col. Lyle B. Otto – Gig Harbor, Washington

1 lb. lean ground venison or
  substitute, crumbled
2 teaspoons seasoned salt
1½ teaspoons ground sage
1½ teaspoons poultry seasoning
1½ teaspoons dried parsley flakes
¼ to ½ teaspoon cayenne
2 tablespoons vegetable oil

8 servings

In medium mixing bowl, combine all ingredients, except oil. Shape mixture into 6-inch log. Wrap in plastic wrap. Refrigerate several hours or overnight.

Slice log into eight ¾-inch-thick patties. In heavy 10-inch nonstick skillet, heat oil over medium heat. Add patties. Cook for 8 to 10 minutes, or until meat is firm and browned, turning patties over once.

Per Serving: Calories: 149 • Protein: 11 g. • Carbohydrate: 0 g. • Fat: 11 g. • Cholesterol: 47 mg. • Sodium: 336 mg. Exchanges: 1½ medium-fat meat, ¾ fat

SMOKING EQUIPMENT AND SUPPLIES include (1) insulated electric smokehouse, with variable-power heat source; (2) electric sheet-aluminum smoker; (3) charcoal or electric water smoker, with water pan above heat source to keep smoker air moist.

INSET: Use (4) wood chips, tree trimmings or smoking sawdust, to provide smoke. Use (5) digital thermometer to monitor internal temperature of salami or large cuts of meat without opening the smoker, which causes heat loss; and (6) instant-read thermometer to monitor smoker temperature; insert thermometer into vent hole on smoker or hole made for thermometer.

Smoking Techniques

Cold smoking is done at temperatures below 120°F, and works well for drying and flavoring jerky and cured sausages, or for flavoring fresh sausages prior to cooking. Hot smoking, or *smoke cooking*, is generally done at temperatures from 150° to 250°F, and is used to fully cook meats while imparting a smoky flavor.

Many types of smokers are available, ranging from sheet-aluminum smokers with an electric hot plate to produce smoke and limited heat, to charcoal or electric-powered water smokers, to insulated variable-temperature smokers. You can also use a covered grill as a hot smoker, or turn an old refrigerator, range or even a garbage can into a smoker. *America's Favorite Fish Recipes, Cleaning & Cooking Fish,* and *Dressing & Cooking Wild Game,* all published by The Hunting & Fishing Library®, go into more detail about these alternative types of smokers.

All smokers require wood to produce smoke. Sports stores and specialty catalogs (see page 128) sell chips and sawdust of various hardwoods, including hickory, cherry, alder, apple and mesquite. You can also use corncobs or hardwood trimmings. Professionals prefer sawdust to larger pieces, because it provides a more even *smudge*. For maximum smoke production, wood chips and trimmings should be soaked in water before use; sawdust should be slightly dampened.

Temperature control is especially important when cooking salami in a smoker, because the salami receives no further cooking. An insulated electric smokehouse is perfect for this, because the temperature is easy to adjust and maintain. Monitor the smoker temperature constantly with an instant-read or oven thermometer. A digital thermometer is useful for monitoring the internal temperature of salami during smoking.

Buffalo Beer Sticks (left)

"Once you taste these, you'll see why they're called beer sticks."
Teresa Marrone – Minneapolis, Minnesota

2	lbs. lean ground buffalo, venison or substitute, crumbled
2	tablespoons Morton® TenderQuick® mix
1½	teaspoons garlic powder
1½	teaspoons onion powder
1	teaspoon freshly ground pepper
½	teaspoon ground coriander
½	teaspoon dry mustard
½	teaspoon cayenne
1½	cups hickory wood chips (optional)
19	mm collagen casing (optional)

32 sticks (about 1 oz. each)

In large nonmetallic mixing bowl, combine all ingredients, except wood chips and casing. Mix by hand until ingredients are evenly distributed. Cover with plastic wrap. Refrigerate 8 hours or overnight.

Place wood chips in large mixing bowl. Cover with water. Soak chips for 1 hour. Place oven thermometer in smoker. Heat smoker until temperature registers 150°F. Drain wood chips.

Stuff casings as directed for natural casings (page 115), using a ½-inch horn and cutting off in 4-inch lengths with sharp knife. (If casings are not used, roll meat mixture by hand into ropes 4 inches long and ½ inch in diameter.)

Arrange beer sticks at least 1 inch apart on smoker racks. Place racks in smoker. Open damper. Place wood chips in smoker. When wood chips begin to smoke, close damper, cracking slightly. Smoke beer sticks at 150° for 1½ to 2¼ hours, or until firm. Cool completely. Store beer sticks, loosely wrapped, in refrigerator for no longer than 1 week, or wrap tightly and freeze up to 2 months.

Variation: To dry beer sticks in conventional oven, add 1 teaspoon liquid smoke flavoring to meat mixture. Continue with recipe as directed, except place oven thermometer in oven. Heat oven to lowest possible temperature setting, propping oven door slightly ajar with wooden spoon to maintain 150°F. Arrange beer sticks on oven racks, spacing as directed. Dry for 1½ to 2¼ hours, or until firm.

Nutritional information not available.

Elk Salami (right)

Rytek Kutas – The Sausage Maker, Buffalo, New York

8 lbs. lean ground elk or substitute, crumbled
2 lbs. pork back fat, cut into 1-inch pieces
2 cups cold water
2 cups soy protein concentrate
¼ cup plus 2 tablespoons canning/pickling salt
2 tablespoons powdered dextrose
2 tablespoons ground nutmeg
1 tablespoon white pepper
2 large cloves garlic, minced
2 level teaspoons Prague Powder No. 1
1½ to 3 cups hickory wood chips
6 to 8 synthetic-fibrous casings, 3½ × 12 inches

About 10 lbs. (2 oz. per serving)

Follow directions below.

Nutritional information not available.

Venison Summer Sausage (middle)

Rytek Kutas – The Sausage Maker, Buffalo, New York

8 lbs. lean ground venison or substitute, crumbled
2 lbs. pork back fat, cut into 1-inch pieces
6 oz. Fermento
¼ cup plus 2 tablespoons canning/ pickling salt
¼ cup powdered dextrose
1 tablespoon freshly ground pepper
1 tablespoon ground coriander
2 level teaspoons Prague Powder No. 1
1 teaspoon ground ginger
1 teaspoon dry mustard
1 teaspoon garlic powder (optional)
1½ to 3 cups hickory wood chips
6 to 8 synthetic-fibrous casings, 3½ × 12 inches

About 10 lbs. (2 oz. per serving)

In large nonmetallic mixing bowl, combine ground meat and back fat. In medium mixing bowl, combine remaining ingredients, except wood chips and casings. Add to meat mixture. Mix by hand until ingredients are evenly distributed. Cover with plastic wrap. Refrigerate 24 hours.

Place wood chips in large mixing bowl. Cover with water. Soak chips for 1 hour. Soak casings as directed for synthetic casings (page 114). Grind meat mixture through a ³⁄₁₆-inch plate. Re-cover meat. Refrigerate until ready to stuff.

Place oven thermometer in smoker. Heat smoker until temperature registers 130°F. Prepare and stuff casings as directed for synthetic casings (page 114), to within 2 inches of top. Secure with butterfly knot as directed for synthetic casings (page 114). If any air pockets remain on surface of sausages, pierce the casing with a sterilized sausage pricker or needle.

Drain wood chips. Hang sausages on smokehouse sticks, spacing at least 1 inch apart. Place in smoker. Open damper. Maintain temperature at 130°F for 30 minutes, or until surface of sausages is dry. Partially close damper to raise temperature to 150°F. Place wood chips in smoker. Smoke at 150°F for 1 hour. Increase temperature to 165°F. Smoke for 5 to 6 hours longer, or until internal temperature of largest sausage registers 152°F. (Times are approximate and will vary, depending upon size and diameter of sausages, weather conditions and type of smoker used.)

Remove sausages from smoker and flush sausages with cold water until internal temperature registers 120°F. Store sausages, tightly wrapped, in refrigerator for no longer than 1 week, or wrap tightly and freeze up to 2 months.

Nutritional information not available.

Smoke-cooked Recipes

The best smokers for *smoke cooking* are water smokers, insulated smokers with temperature control or covered charcoal grills. Follow the recipe for smoke-cooking time, and then check the meat for doneness. If it isn't done after the allotted time, finish cooking in a 325°F oven.

To use a covered grill for smoke cooking, pile briquettes along two sides of a round grill, or in one corner of a square grill. For water smoking, place a pan of water between the hot coal beds, or on the grate above the coals in a square grill. Put the meat to be smoked on the grate in the center of the grill, above the water pan (in a square grill, place the meat on the grate in the corner opposite the coals).

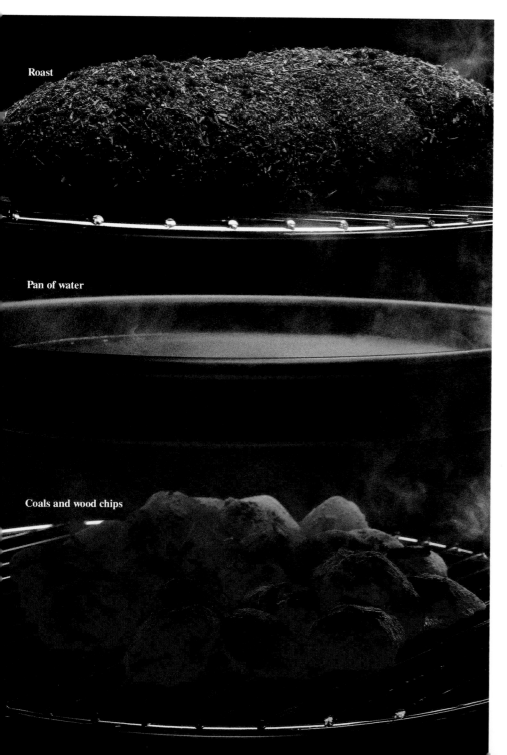

Roast

Pan of water

Coals and wood chips

Buttery Smoked Pheasant with Onions

Teresa Marrone – Minneapolis, Minnesota

¼ cup butter, melted
½ teaspoon sugar
½ teaspoon dry mustard
½ teaspoon salt
¼ teaspoon paprika
⅛ teaspoon cayenne
1 dressed pheasant or substitute (1½ to 2¼ lbs), cut up, skin removed
1½ cups apple or cherry wood chips
1 medium onion, sliced

3 or 4 servings

In medium mixing bowl, combine all ingredients, except pheasant pieces, wood chips and onion. Add pheasant pieces, turning to coat. Cover with plastic wrap. Chill 1 hour.

Meanwhile, place wood chips in large mixing bowl. Cover with water. Soak chips for 1 hour. Place oven thermometer in smoker. Heat smoker until temperature registers 250°F. Drain wood chips.

Arrange onion slices in bottom of 9-inch square disposable foil baking pan. Arrange pheasant pieces over onion. Remelt any remaining butter mixture and pour over pheasant pieces.

Place pan on top rack of smoker. Open damper. Place wood chips in smoker. When wood chips begin to smoke, close damper, cracking slightly. Smoke pheasant pieces for 1½ to 2 hours at 250°F, or until juices run clear. Serve pheasant with onion and pan drippings.

Per Serving: Calories: 454 • Protein: 42 g.
• Carbohydrate: 4 g. • Fat: 29 g.
• Cholesterol: 31 mg. • Sodium: 465 mg.
Exchanges: 5¼ medium-fat meat,
1 vegetable, ¾ fat

Smoked Buffalo with Red Chili Honey Chutney

"I smoke the roast and then finish it on the grill because I use this recipe on our Saturday cookout, so we prep at the kitchen and take the food to one of our lakes for a barbecue cookout."
Mark A. Nimon, Executive Chef – Vermejo Park Ranch, Raton, New Mexico

CHUTNEY:

1½ cups Major Gray's Chutney®
 1 cup lingonberry preserves
 ⅓ cup honey
 2 tablespoons chili powder
 1 teaspoon salt
 1 teaspoon pepper

1½ cups hickory wood chips
 1 tablespoon paprika
 2 to 3 cloves garlic, minced
 2 teaspoons coarsely ground pepper
 1 teaspoon dried marjoram leaves
 1 teaspoon dried thyme leaves
 1 teaspoon dried rosemary leaves
 1 teaspoon onion salt
 5 lbs. boneless buffalo rib eye roast, elk loin or substitute, well trimmed

18 servings

In food processor or blender, combine all chutney ingredients. Process until smooth. Cover. Set aside. Place wood chips in large mixing bowl. Cover with water. Soak chips for 1 hour.

In small mixing bowl, combine remaining ingredients, except buffalo. Rub seasoning mixture evenly over roast. Place oven thermometer in smoker. Heat smoker until temperature registers 200°F. Spray smoker rack with nonstick vegetable cooking spray. Place roast on rack. Place in center of smoker. Open damper and maintain 200°F for 1 hour to dry surface of roast. (If juices are released from roast during this time, temperature is too high.) Drain wood chips. Place wood chips in smoker. When wood chips begin to smoke, close damper, cracking slightly. Smoke roast for 1 hour at 200°F. Remove roast from smoker.

On charcoal grill or in preheated 325°F oven, finish cooking roast to desired doneness. Remove from grill. Let roast stand, tented with foil, for 10 minutes before carving. Carve roast across grain into thin slices. Serve with chutney.

Per Serving: Calories: 312 • Protein: 29 g. • Carbohydrate: 34 g. • Fat: 6 g. • Cholesterol: 55 mg. • Sodium: 518 mg.
Exchanges: 4 lean meat, 2 fruit

Texas Fowl

Eddy Mayfield – Red Bluff Shooting Preserve, Trent, Texas

 1 can (12 oz.) beer, divided
 3 tablespoons peach preserves
 2 tablespoons soy sauce
 1 tablespoon red pepper sauce
 ¼ teaspoon garlic salt
 ⅛ teaspoon pepper
 8 boneless skinless whole quail breasts (1½ oz. each), split in half
1½ cups mesquite wood chips
 4 small jalapeño peppers, each cut in half lengthwise and seeded
 8 slices bacon
 2 tablespoons Catalina dressing
 1 tablespoon catsup
 1 tablespoon Worcestershire sauce
1½ teaspoons lime juice
 ½ teaspoon chili powder

8 servings

In medium mixing bowl, combine 1¼ cups beer, the preserves, soy sauce, red pepper sauce, garlic salt and pepper. Add breast halves. Stir to coat. Cover with plastic wrap. Refrigerate 24 hours.

Place wood chips in large mixing bowl. Cover with water. Soak chips for 1 hour. Place oven thermometer in smoker. Heat smoker until temperature registers 250°F. Spray smoker rack with nonstick vegetable cooking spray. Set aside.

Drain and discard marinade from quail breast halves. Place 1 pepper half between 2 breast halves. Wrap with 1 slice bacon. Secure with wooden pick. Repeat with remaining breast halves, pepper halves and bacon slices.

In small mixing bowl, combine remaining ¼ cup beer, the dressing, catsup, Worcestershire sauce, juice and chili powder. Set baste aside.

Drain wood chips. Arrange quail bundles at least 2 inches apart on prepared rack. Place in center of smoker. Open damper. Place wood chips in smoker. When wood chips begin to smoke, close damper, cracking slightly. Smoke quail bundles for 1 to 1½ hours at 250°F, or until juices run clear, brushing with baste twice during smoking. Garnish with sliced fresh jalapeño peppers, if desired.

Per Serving: Calories: 112 • Protein: 11 g. • Carbohydrate: 4 g. • Fat: 6 g. • Cholesterol: 5 mg. • Sodium: 283 mg.
Exchanges: 1 medium-fat meat, 1 vegetable

Jerky

When old-time drovers killed an animal, they would "jerk" the tenderloins from the carcass, then hang the meat over a smoky fire until it was dry and preserved.

Any lean game meat without tendons or sinews can be used to make jerky, except that from bear, boar or javelina, which must be thoroughly cooked. Cut meat with the grain for a chewy texture; or across the grain for a more tender jerky.

Traditionally, jerky is smoked, but it can also be flavored with liquid smoke and dried in a cool oven (directions opposite) or dehydrator.

Use a curing salt like Morton® TenderQuick® mix when preparing jerky, to help prevent bacterial growth.

Dakota Jack Hot Venison Jerky (left)

Richard R. Roinestad – Phoenix, Arizona

MARINADE:
- 1 can (12 oz.) beer
- 1 cup cold water
- 1/3 cup soy sauce
- 3 tablespoons Morton® TenderQuick® mix
- 2 tablespoons crushed peppercorns
- 2 pepperoncini peppers, broken
- 1 tablespoon pepperoncini juice
- 1 tablespoon hot chili oil
- 1 tablespoon red pepper sauce
- 1 tablespoon dried onion flakes
- 1 tablespoon crushed red pepper flakes
- 1 teaspoon Cajun seasoning
- 1/4 teaspoon garlic powder

- 2 lbs. boneless venison rump or substitute, cut into 4 × 1 × 1/4-inch strips
- 1 1/2 to 3 cups hickory wood chips

11 servings (40 to 50 slices)

Follow directions on opposite page.

Per Serving: Calories: 107 • Protein: 19 g.
• Carbohydrate: 1 g. • Fat: 2 g.
• Cholesterol: 70 mg. • Sodium: 499 mg.
Exchanges: 2 lean meat, 1/4 vegetable

Turkey Jerky (middle)

Larry Whiteley – Springfield, Missouri

MARINADE:
- 3 1/2 cups cold water
- 3 tablespoons Morton® TenderQuick® mix
- 2 tablespoons Worcestershire sauce
- 2 tablespoons soy sauce
- 1 1/2 teaspoons onion powder
- 1/2 teaspoon garlic powder
- 1/2 teaspoon pepper

- 2 lbs. boneless skinless wild turkey breast, cut into 4 × 1 × 1/4-inch strips
- 1 1/2 to 3 cups apple wood chips

11 servings (40 to 50 slices)

Follow directions on opposite page.

Per Serving: Calories: 93 • Protein: 20 g.
• Carbohydrate: 0 g. • Fat: 1 g.
• Cholesterol: 51 mg. • Sodium: 396 mg.
Exchanges: 2 lean meat

Wild Bill's Venison Jerky (right)

Jerry L. Smalley – Columbia Falls, Montana

MARINADE:
- 4 cups cold water
- 3 tablespoons Morton® TenderQuick® mix
- 2 tablespoons Worcestershire sauce
- 1 tablespoon soy sauce
- 1 tablespoon freshly ground pepper
- 1 teaspoon garlic powder
- 1/2 teaspoon red pepper sauce

- 2 lbs. boneless venison round steak or substitute, cut into 4 × 1 × 1/4-inch strips
- 1 1/2 to 3 cups hickory wood chips

11 servings (40 to 50 slices)

Follow directions on opposite page.

Per Serving: Calories: 101 • Protein: 19 g.
• Carbohydrate: 1 g. • Fat: 2 g.
• Cholesterol: 70 mg. • Sodium: 376 mg.
Exchanges: 2 lean meat

How to Make Jerky

USE a special slicing board (see page 128 for mail-order source) and a very sharp knife to ensure even thickness of meat strips. The lip along the edges and a special insert board help guide the knife. Meat is easier to slice if it is partially frozen.

SPRAY smoker racks with nonstick vegetable cooking spray. Set aside. Drain wood chips. Drain and discard marinade from meat strips. Pat strips lightly with paper towels. Arrange strips at least ¼ inch apart on prepared racks. Place racks in smoker.

Oven Method for Making Jerky

ADD 2 teaspoons liquid smoke flavoring to marinade. Continue with recipe as directed, except place oven thermometer in oven. Heat oven to lowest possible temperature setting, propping oven door with wooden spoon so it is open about 7 inches at top to maintain 120°F.

COMBINE marinade ingredients in large nonmetallic mixing bowl. Stir to dissolve salt. Add meat strips. Cover with plastic wrap. Refrigerate 24 hours, stirring occasionally. In large mixing bowl, cover wood chips with water. Soak for 1 hour. Place oven thermometer in smoker. Heat smoker to 120°F.

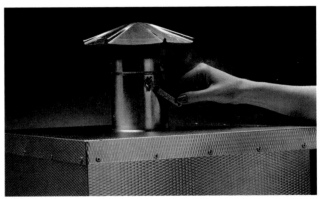

OPEN damper. Place a handful of wood chips in smoker. Close damper, cracking slightly when wood chips begin to smoke. Smoke meat strips for 3 to 6 hours, or until dry but not brittle, adding wood chips as necessary. Cool completely. Store jerky, loosely wrapped, in refrigerator for no longer than 1 week, or wrap tightly and freeze up to 2 months.

SPRAY four 14 × 10-inch cooling racks with nonstick vegetable cooking spray. Arrange meat strips on prepared racks, spacing as directed. Dry for 3 to 4 hours, or until dry but not brittle.

123

Index

Cy DeCosse Incorporated offers a variety of
how-to books. For information write:

Cy DeCosse Subscriber Books
5900 Green Oak Drive
Minnetonka, MN 55343